Chicago Gourmet

BY

SUE KUPCINET AND CONNIE FISH

A FIRESIDE BOOK PUBLISHED BY
SIMON AND SCHUSTER

COPYRIGHT © 1977 BY SUE KUPCINET AND CONNIE FISH
ALL RIGHTS RESERVED
INCLUDING THE RIGHT OF REPRODUCTION
IN WHOLE OR IN PART IN ANY FORM
A FIRESIDE BOOK
PUBLISHED BY SIMON AND SCHUSTER
A DIVISION OF GULF & WESTERN CORPORATION
SIMON & SCHUSTER BUILDING
ROCKEFELLER CENTER
1230 AVENUE OF THE AMERICAS
NEW YORK, NEW YORK 10020

DESIGNED BY EVE METZ
MANUFACTURED IN THE UNITED STATES OF AMERICA

1 2 3 4 5 6 7 8 9 10
LIBRARY OF CONGRESS CATALOGING IN PUBLICATION DATA
KUPCINET, SUE.
    CHICAGO GOURMET.

    (A FIRESIDE BOOK)
    INCLUDES INDEX.
    1. CHICAGO—RESTAURANTS—DIRECTORIES.   I. FISH,
CONNIE, JOINT AUTHOR.   II. TITLE.
TX907.K86   647'.95773'11   77-11041
ISBN 0-671-22896-X

Contents

v

CONTENTS

vi

vii

CONTENTS

CONTENTS

CONTENTS

Foreword

Omar Khayyam said it best: "A Jug of Wine, a Loaf of Bread—and Thou." Thus he commingled man's strongest drives—drink, food and sex. This delightful book on Chicago cuisine tackles the first two (two out of three ain't bad) and leaves the third to others.

Sue Kupcinet and Connie Fish may well be the counterparts of Ann Landers and Abbie Van Buren in giving advice. They have devoted themselves to appraising and recommending the finest restaurants in Chicago. They also offer the favorite recipes of the chefs they interviewed.

This was not an easy task, as this columnist of more than three decades, who has been wined and dined from coast to coast, can testify. Chicago ranks among the finest dining cities in the nation. Right up there with New York, New Orleans, San Francisco and Los Angeles, which are considered, though not exclusively, the *haute cuisine* centers of the United States.

Sue and Connie tackled their assignment with a youthful vigor that is refreshing. Their intent is to provide a guide to distinctive dining, where the food, wine and service all mesh for a delightful evening.

They go one step further by dealing with another important matter in dining out. That's the price you may expect to pay for the pleasure of your palate.

They did their job with a professionalism that would please an old newspaperman. They visited every restaurant named in this book without advance warning to owner or maitre d' to avoid special attention and to make sure you will be treated as they were. They also tested every recipe offered herein.

To give their book breadth and depth, they did not limit their visits to the "in" spots which cater to VIPs and celebrities. They also went to the neighborhood ethnic restaurants, suburban restaurants and Ma-and-Pa restaurants. Few cities can match the delights of the Chicago ethnics, from French to Italian to Latino to Chinese to Polish to Bohemian to Soul.

I know and can vouch for the efforts of Sue Kupcinet and Connie Fish. Sue happens to be my daughter-in-law and if this sounds like nepotism, I can only quote the words of our late Mayor Richard Daley: "What's wrong with nepotism, as long as you keep it in the family?" The fact that she is my daughter-in-law also means I know first-hand how industriously she and Connie worked on this effort.

IRV KUPCINET
Chicago Sun-Times

Chicago Gourmet

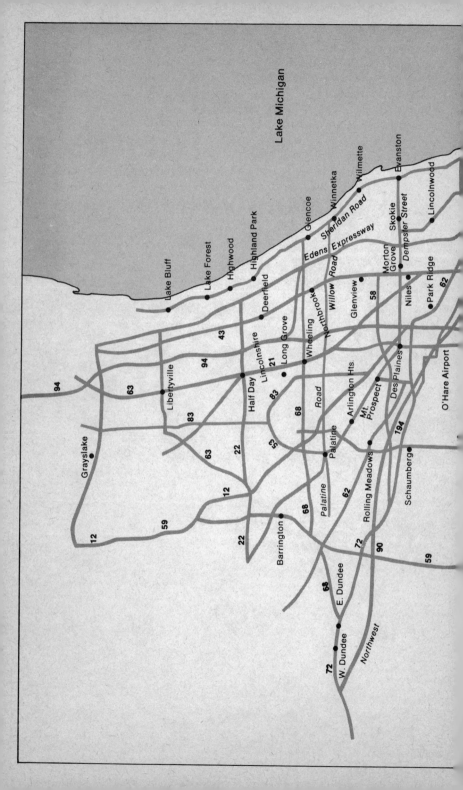

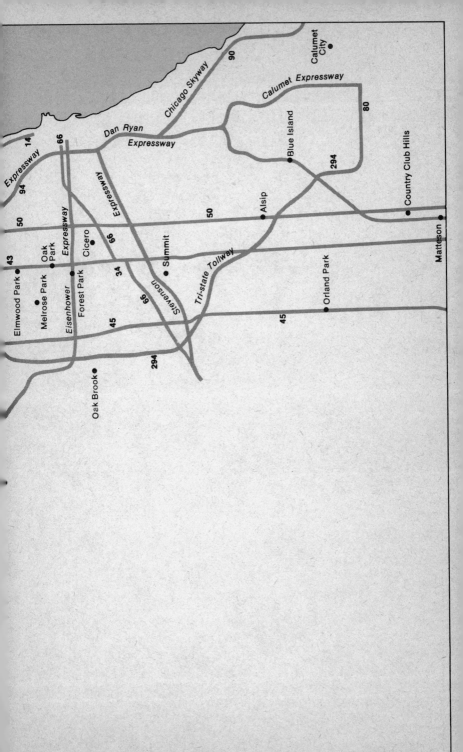

Introduction

Chicago, your selective restaurant and recipe guide is here! The information compiled in this book will answer the many questions commonly asked about dining out as well as dining in. Hopefully it will eliminate the rut that we all tend to get into and increase your dining experiences. Our town is made up of a great many ethnic backgrounds, providing us with restaurants offering a wide variety of foods and decor. After eating at each restaurant and testing the recipes provided, we have expanded our tastes as well as our waistlines.

The restaurants listed were carefully chosen for their excellence; the diner who loves good food, good service and pleasant ambiance can choose at a glance from the wide range included.

Our book originated with the simple question, "Where should we go for dinner?" Pleasantly surprised at the many excellent choices that exist in the Chicago and suburban areas, we realized that we have one of the most complete and finest dining areas in the country. This information is what we want to share with you. Also, we'd like to share the superb recipes that we've collected from the chefs at each restaurant. They have been kitchen tested, by us, and enjoyed by our friends and families.

Our wine consultant, Mr. E. Leonard Solomon, has written a chapter to familiarize you with the basic knowledge of wine and wine etiquette in restaurants. He has also given his personal suggestions of wine to accompany each recipe, when appropriate.

For your convenience, we have indexed our restaurants in three ways.

1. Location—This will give an idea of what's available in your vicinity or one that you're willing to travel to.

2. Cuisine—When a certain taste is what you're looking for, this index will aid you in finding that particular food.

3. Dinner price range—Prices change, but our intention is to give you an approximate idea of what your evening will cost. The price per person includes an appetizer or soup, salad, entree, dessert and coffee. It does not include cocktails, wine or gratuities. Also included is an index of recipes from each restaurant for entertaining, Chicago style, in your home.

The keys to the credit cards are as follows; AE (American Express); CB (Carte Blanche); DC (Diners Club); MC (Master Charge); VI (Visa; formerly BankAmericard).

Now look through our guide and plan your next night out or your next night in. Enjoy and Eat, Chicago, Eat!

SUE KUPCINET AND CONNIE FISH

The Silent Sommelier

by E. Leonard Solomon

Wine has been important in the history of mankind since its earliest beginnings. It has always been a social beverage, bringing solace and pleasure to rich and poor alike. Wine is an adjunct to gracious living . . . you can live without wine, but *with* wine you live!

"The art of drinking is the art of eating . . . they are one and the same!" The purpose of this chapter is to offer some basic wine knowledge, suggestions for judging the wine value of a restaurant, the patron's Bill of Rights, and some expression of the restaurateur's rights.

It is gratifying to see that forty-four years after the penalty of prohibition, wine is assuming its rightful place on the table as a casual food—not always relegated to specific celebrations or reserved for religious observances. It is also a positive factor that the development of American wines is proceeding rapidly, not in imitation of their European cousins, but in their own right. Of course, comparisons will always be made, but California wines should be judged uniquely, as should the wines of New York, Missouri, Ohio or Washington, rather than generically. (Generic means with reference to a European regional counterpart, e.g., Chablis, Burgundy, Rhine, Sauterne.)

"To cocktail or not to cocktail" is often the question. The answer is simple. Several high-proof drinks will numb the taste buds and you will not be able to appreciate either the wines or the food that will follow. A very dry Fino sherry, or Manzanilla, or an aperitif such as Lillet Blonde, or a dry white wine that you

3

will continue into the first course, will properly prepare you for the tastes to come. Champagne is the one wine that you can drink from aperitif through dessert!

As far as the order of drinking wines is concerned, if you have more than one—and it's fun not to have two bottles of the same wine, but to vary and experiment—the rules are: dry before sweet, white before red, younger before older, lesser before greater. There are certain classic food and wine marriages tested over the centuries, just as apple pie and ice cream, ham and eggs, and bacon, lettuce and tomato are happy combinations. Our one rule is that there is seldom a time when a dry white wine will not go better with fish than a red, unless the fish is cooked with tomato and spices. The tannin in red wine is not compatible with fish oils.

Certainly taste is personal, and if you like chocolate with oysters, enjoy it! But we wouldn't recommend that liaison as a great taste experience. The purpose of wine with food is that neither overwhelms but enhances the other. The resultant happy goal is called "gourmet." "Gourmet" can be an expertly boiled egg or a perfect strawberry. What we call "gourmet" does not have to be complicated or expensive. An inexpensive glass of sound wine can be "gourmet" as well as the most expensive wine.

Here are some parameters for judging the wine value of a restaurant:

    1. Does it have a sufficiently extensive but uncomplicated wine list with enough variety, not exorbitantly priced? A good restaurant will price its wines at twice wholesale. This enables the establishment of a sufficient cellar to afford continuity of wines so as not to have to say continually, "Sorry, we're out of that." Most lists are priced at twice the normal retail price and then some! There is a tendency now for intelligent owners of restaurants to price their lists at the regular retail price, just as in a store, offering no penalty to the consumer. Bless them! Neither you nor I like to be taken advantage of just because we like wine with our food.

    2. Are the selections of wines suitable to the food of-

fered in the restaurant? Offering only "jug" wines with *haute cuisine* is a mistake. So is offering only great red Bordeaux with spicy Mexican foods.

3. Is the wine service proper and unobtrusive? The current trend in service is to eliminate the sommelier or wine steward, making each waiter responsible for the serving of wine. This saves you an extra tip, which money really goes toward the price of the wine. Your waiter will be more attentive than a sommelier, because it is his table and he can respond quickly to your needs. The waiter should be knowledgeable about the wines on the list of his own restaurant . . . he doesn't have to be a wine expert in general. The waiter should know how to present, open and pour the wine correctly. He should be helpful, not haughty; informative, not intimidating. The glassware should be sparkling clean and clean glasses should be supplied for each different wine. Wine glasses should never be poured more than half full. Wine chillers at tableside are not an affectation; wine cradles, unless for a very old wine that you have ordered ahead, are not necessary. Even if you have chosen some ancient bottle days ahead, the wine should probably have been decanted.

4. Tipping is a personal matter. Without the wine steward, normal custom prevails and nothing extra has to be added for wine service. If there is a sommelier, one dollar per bottle is sufficient.

There usually will be a common denominator permitting the selection of a particular wine when several dining companions order different main courses. If there is not, remember that restaurants are offering excellent wines by the glass in order to stimulate the sale of wine. It's one way to satisfy everybody. Taste cautiously, however, to see if the wine is sound. If there isn't enough turnover, the wine may have been open too long. If a dry white wine tastes sherry-like or is brownish in color, you will know it's oxidized and faulty. A red wine is unsound if it smells of acetic acid (vinegar).

It is fun to experiment at home so that you can become acquainted with imperfection as well as perfection. You can learn as much from a bad bottle of wine as you can from a good bottle. Your Bill of Rights always asserts that you may legitimately complain. A good restaurant will never argue, but replace the wine. If it's a hundred-dollar bottle of a great wine, however, an intense discussion may result.

On behalf of the restaurateur, if the wine you are served is sound, but not quite as good as you expected, realize that we drink from bottle to bottle and not from case to case . . . have some compassion. And don't say that a wine is "corked" if a careless waiter inadvertently permits a little cork crumb in the host's glass when the wine is offered for initial approval. A "corked" wine is one that has a mildewy or musty smell. Strange smells are always evident in wines that have just been opened. The purpose of the waiter's taking the wine order at the same time the food is ordered is so that the wine will have a chance to aerate or breathe for half an hour. (See any good wine books for explanation.)

When in doubt, order a "house" or carafe wine. The quality is generally good and usually enough is sold so that it hasn't been opened or refrigerated for days! French wines are often poured from magnums (double bottles) and are usually most pleasant.

"A meal well conceived is like a symphony well conducted." Search out the restaurants into which you may bring your own wines. Even if a small corkage charge is imposed, it's worth it. If you call in advance, restaurants with regular wine lists will usually permit you to bring something special. With some forethought, you will have the unique experience of DINING and not just eating.

Bon Appetit!

The Restaurants

(AND THEIR SPECIALTIES)

THE ABACUS

ADDRESS   2619 North Clark Street
TELEPHONE   248–6700
HOURS AND DAYS   Lunch: Mon.–Sat. 11:30 A.M.–2:30 P.M.
   Dinner: Mon.–Thurs. 5–11 P.M.;
   Fri., Sat. 5 P.M.–midnight;
   Sun. 1–11 P.M.
HOLIDAYS CLOSED   Thanksgiving, Christmas
RESERVATIONS   Recommended
CREDIT CARDS   AE, MC, VI
ENTERTAINMENT   No
PARKING   At 2569 North Clark
BANQUET FACILITIES   Yes
DRESS   Casual
LIQUOR   Yes
WINE   Small selection

The Abacus is truly a gourmet Chinese restaurant. It offers Cantonese, Mandarin, Shanghai and spicy Szechwan selections. Red is the predominant color used in the many Oriental fixtures. A lazy Susan is placed in the center of each table to aid in the custom of sharing each dish. Everyone should start his or her meal with the giant-sized egg roll. It's fabulous. The pork in Mandarin Pancakes and the Cantonese Lemon Chicken proved to be good choices for the entree. An excellent finish was the Sugar Spun Apple, a very tasty and unusual dessert.

8

Dr. Shen's Barbecued Spareribs

Serves 4–6

2 pounds spareribs
1 teaspoon five-spice powder, or allspice
½ cup dark soy sauce
2 tablespoons light soy sauce
3 tablespoons honey
1½ cups hoisin sauce

2 tablespoons Chinese rice wine (or pale dry sherry)
1 tablespoon white vinegar
¼ teaspoon chopped garlic
½ cup sugar
½ cup tomato catsup
1 teaspoon Worcestershire sauce
¼ cup chicken broth

Remove skirt and tough membrane on back side of ribs by inserting a prong of a fork under it and peeling it off. Fill a kettle with enough water to immerse the spareribs. Bring water to a boil, then add the spareribs with five-spice powder and again allow to boil. Simmer until a two-pronged fork can easily pass through, but meat is still firm. Combine all the remaining ingredients. Mix well. The marinade can be stored in the refrigerator for several months. Remove the ribs from kettle and immerse them in the marinade while hot. Let stand for at least half an hour, or overnight. Preheat oven to 450°. Place spareribs on roasting pan with bone side up and bake, basting them frequently with marinade. Turn ribs over after five minutes and set oven to broil. Broil meat side until reddish brown. To serve, cut the spareribs into individual pieces.

This recipe can also be used with barbecued chicken or pork.

Wine suggestion: Medium red Italian wine

AL FARBER'S STEAK ROOM

ADDRESS   2300 North Lincoln Park West
TELEPHONE   525-7375
HOURS AND DAYS   Daily 5 P.M.–1 A.M.
HOLIDAYS CLOSED   Thanksgiving, Christmas
RESERVATIONS   Yes
CREDIT CARDS   All major cards
ENTERTAINMENT   No
PARKING   Doorman
BANQUET FACILITIES   Up to 75
DRESS   Informal
LIQUOR   Yes
WINE   Ample wine list

Al Farber's is famous for "Eye of Prime Rib" and its unique charcrust steaks. This popular restaurant, facing Lincoln Park, has received many awards, including The Perfect Steak Award, the Epicurean Award, the Red Sheep Seal Award, and the Gourmet Society Merit Award. Their new offering is a five-course Continental Dinner, which includes soup, salad, entree, potato and dessert. This offer is "Never on Sunday." Any day, however, the steaks and chops are consistently great. Their special baked potato, blended with butter and eggs and topped with sour cream and chives, is an added touch that everyone enjoys.

Al Farber's Famous Cabbage Soup

Serves 10

Liquid or powdered beef
stock concentrate to make
1 quart stock
¼ pound beef chuck, cut in
1" cubes
½ pound white cabbage,
shredded

1 whole red tomato
1 small onion, diced
1 tablespoon sour salt (citric
acid)
¼ pound sugar
1 pinch salt

Add water to the beef stock concentrate to equal 1 quart and put in large pot with other ingredients. Simmer two hours over medium heat, adding salt and sugar as desired. Set aside for three hours. Reheat to serve.

This soup also can be frozen for future use.

Drink suggestion: Pilsner Urquell beer

ALLGAUER'S FIRESIDE

ADDRESS   2855 Milwaukee Avenue, Northbrook
TELEPHONE   541-6000
HOURS AND DAYS   Daily 11 A.M.–1 A.M.
HOLIDAYS CLOSED   July 4
RESERVATIONS   Preferred
CREDIT CARDS   AE, DC, MC, VI
ENTERTAINMENT   Tues.–Sat. in Cocktail Lounge
PARKING   Yes
BANQUET FACILITIES   From 25 to 800
DRESS   Semi-formal
LIQUOR   Yes
WINE   Good selection

A magnificent contemporary restaurant, in colors of browns, rusts, and beiges, Allgauer's has a beautiful view, from the dining room, overlooking the Des Plaines River and Forest Preserves. A large fireplace and a sunken conversation pit give you an opportunity to be comfortable while you have a drink. There is also an atrium available for cocktails, and a banquet area that features an outdoor cocktail patio in rustic wooded surroundings. Allgauer's has been in business for forty years, and their success is due to their belief in high quality. Suggestions for ordering are crab legs, Tournedos Tivoli (sautéed twin petite filet mignons, with béarnaise sauce), Rystafel (shrimp, crabmeat and medallions of lobster blended together in a mild curry sauce, served on a bed of saffron rice) and their delicious Black Forest Torte for dessert.

Coquilles St. Jacques

Serves 3

45 scallops
½ cup sauterne wine
½ cup water
4 ounces (½ cup) fresh
   sliced mushrooms
   Pinch each of salt and
   celery seed
6 black peppercorns
3 tablespoons clarified
   butter

3 tablespoons flour
½ cup cream
1 egg yolk
   Grated Parmesan cheese
1 cup mashed potatoes
   (made from 2 medium
   potatoes, 2 tablespoons
   each butter and cream,
   salt and pepper)

You will need one large mother-of-pearl scallop shell for each serving.

Poach scallops in wine and water with mushrooms and seasonings for 5 minutes. Strain; reserve liquid and scallops. Blend 2 tablespoons butter and flour and cook to make a roux; add liquid from scallops to make cream sauce. Add cream to sauce and beat in the egg yolk for color. Finish with 2 tablespoons Parmesan cheese. Put a border of mashed potatoes around each scallop shell; add 15 scallops in the center of each shell. Cover with sauce, sprinkle with grated Parmesan cheese and 1 tablespoon butter. Place in an oven at 350° and bake for 8 to 10 minutes or until brown. Serve immediately.

Wine suggestion: Spanish dry sherry

ANN SATHER'S

ADDRESS   925 West Belmont Avenue
TELEPHONE   348-2378
HOURS AND DAYS   Mon.–Thurs. 11 A.M.–8 P.M.;
        Sun. noon–7 P.M.
HOLIDAYS CLOSED   All major holidays except Easter and
        Mother's Day
RESERVATIONS   No
CREDIT CARDS   No
ENTERTAINMENT   No
PARKING   No
BANQUET FACILITIES   No
DRESS   Casual
LIQUOR   No
WINE   No

Beautiful Swedish needlepoint pictures and shelves of interesting knick-knacks add to the charm and warmth felt at Ann Sather's. Scandinavian food is the specialty, but all types are served. Dinners include a choice of soup or appetizer, freshly made breads, salad, entree, vegetables, beverage and homemade desserts in an unbelievable $3.35–$6 price range. The homemade breads and desserts are freshly made daily and fantastically good!

Lamb Stew in Dill Sauce

Serves 4–6

4 *pounds lamb shoulder, cut*
  for stew with bone
Salt to taste
4 *whole allspice*

½ *cup chopped onion*
¼ *cup fresh dill, stems and*
  leaves, chopped
Flour

Cover meat completely with water and add all remaining ingredients except flour. Bring to a boil and let simmer 1½ hours in a covered pot. Test meat. When tender, remove the meat. Thicken gravy to consistency you like, using a smooth mixture of flour and water. You may tint with yellow food coloring if desired. Add meat to gravy. Serve with fluffy dumplings. Boiled potatoes and pickled beets go well with this stew.
Wine suggestion: Medium white California wine

ARNIE'S

ADDRESS   1030 North State Street (and 1876 First Street,
    Highland Park)
TELEPHONE   266-4800
HOURS AND DAYS   Lunch: Mon.–Fri. 11:30 A.M.–2:30 P.M.;
    Sun. brunch 11 A.M.–2:30 P.M.
    Dinner: Mon.–Thurs. 5:30–11 P.M.;
    Fri. 5:30–11:30 P.M.;
    Sat. 5:30 P.M.–12:30 A.M.
HOLIDAYS CLOSED   All national holidays
RESERVATIONS   Yes
CREDIT CARDS   AE, DC, MC, VI
ENTERTAINMENT   Stanley Paul and his Orchestra, Tues.–Sat.
    from 6 P.M.
PARKING   On premises
BANQUET FACILITIES   Wicker Room—Parties up to 100
DRESS   Casual elegance
LIQUOR   Until 2 A.M. weekdays, 3 A.M. Sat.
WINE   Good selection

    The latest rage with Chicago's contemporary crowd, Arnie's is a unique dining spa in which good Continental cuisine and an elegant atmosphere add up to an exceptional experience. *Vogue* magazine called Arnie's "The magically flamboyant Chicago restaurant, where they're packing them in because of the million-dollar decor, a boggling mix of Art Nouveau and Art Deco." Try the Veal Florentine (thin slices of veal over spinach, covered with Mornay Sauce) or pepper steak, and don't forget to include a tasty spinach salad. A more casual menu is offered at Arnie's new addition, a sophisticated glass-enclosed outdoor cafe. It's a fun place to practice the sport of people-watching.

Sirloin Steak Arnie's

Serves 4

4 New York sirloin steaks   ½ cup béarnaise sauce
  (10 ounces each)   (bottled or own recipe)
8-ounce can lobster meat

Broil steaks to taste. Place 2 ounces of lobster meat on each steak. Cover entire steak and lobster with béarnaise sauce. Place under broiler until glazed and serve immediately.
Wine suggestion: California or Rhône dry rosé

THE ATRIUM

ADDRESS   3223 West Algonquin Road (2 blocks off Route 53), Rolling Meadows
TELEPHONE   259-7070; Chicago number 763-0150
HOURS AND DAYS   Lunch: Mon.–Thurs. and Sun. 11 A.M.–2 P.M.
Lounge open all afternoon
Dinner: Weekdays 4:30–11:45 P.M.;
Weekends 4:30 P.M.–12:45 A.M.
HOLIDAYS CLOSED   Christmas, New Year's Day
RESERVATIONS   Yes
CREDIT CARDS   All major cards
ENTERTAINMENT   Tues.–Sat.
PARKING   Yes
BANQUET FACILITIES   Dining Room on Sat. until 4:30 P.M.
DRESS   Jacket suggested
LIQUOR   Yes
WINE   Good wine list

Here's a restaurant where you can surround yourself with elaborate decor. The flowing fountains complete the elegant picture. We recommend the Caesar Salad, the fantastic trout stuffed with crabmeat, and the specialty of the house, Veal Oscar à la Waldorf. The service is excellent and they bend over backwards to please you. Located three minutes from the Arlington Park Theater, they will make sure you catch the show on time.

Veal Oscar à la Waldorf

Serves 1

1 ounce medallion from
boned white leg of veal
2 eggs
2 tablespoons milk
Flour
Butter

2 ounces chopped king
crabmeat
Béarnaise sauce (own or
bottled)
Madeira sauce (see below)

Meat should be completely defatted and deveined. Place between pieces of wax paper and flatten with flat end of cleaver. Dip into mixture of eggs and milk, then coat with flour. Sauté lightly in butter in aluminum skillet for 30 seconds on each side. Place skillet in 450° oven for 4 minutes. Remove and sprinkle with crabmeat. Cover it all with béarnaise sauce. Return to broiler until very lightly browned. Top with a drizzling of Madeira sauce. Serve with wild rice.

SPAÑOLA SAUCE BASE/MADEIRA SAUCE

2–3 pounds veal bones
1 cup celery, peeled and
diced
1 cup onions, peeled and
chopped
1 cup carrots, peeled and
chopped
⅛ teaspoon rosemary leaves
1 small can tomato purée
1 small can tomato sauce
2 cups flour
3 cups water
⅛ teaspoon peppercorns

3 leeks
1 bay leaf
⅛ teaspoon crushed red
pepper flakes
Small pinch of thyme
½ teaspoon oregano
2 cloves of garlic, split
⅛ teaspoon margarine
Salt to taste
½ cup Madeira wine
1 shallot, diced
½ leek
3 tablespoons butter

Place veal bones in a cast-iron pot and brown in 450° oven for 35 minutes. Add celery, onions and carrots, rosemary leaves, tomato puree and tomato sauce. With these ingredients on top of bones, roast for an additional 10 minutes. After the first 5 minutes, add 2 cups flour and let set for the last 5 minutes. At this point, transfer to a double boiler and add water. Add peppercorns, 3 leeks, bay leaf, red pepper flakes, thyme, oregano, garlic, margarine, and salt to taste; boil for 4 hours.

To prepare for Veal Oscar:

Add ¼ cup Madeira wine, shallot and ½ leek. Allow to boil for 10 minutes and add another ¼ cup of wine. Strain into large bowl and place pats of butter on top to prevent skin from forming. Refrigerate until needed.

Wine suggestion: Medium white Alsatian wine

THE BAKERY

ADDRESS   2218 North Lincoln Avenue
TELEPHONE   472-6942
HOURS AND DAYS   Tues.–Sat. 5 P.M.–midnight
HOLIDAYS CLOSED   Christmas, New Year's Day
RESERVATIONS   Yes
CREDIT CARDS   No
ENTERTAINMENT   No
PARKING   Street
BANQUET FACILITIES   Up to 80
DRESS   Casual
LIQUOR   No
WINE   Good selection

Founded 15 years ago, The Bakery was a store-front restaurant where the emphasis has always been on food and service, not on decor. The chef owner, Louis Szathmary, has held
to his philosophy—that beautiful women are the real interior
decoration. Although unpretentious, The Bakery uses all silver
service—no stainless steel, plastic flowers or canned foods are
tolerated. Chef Louis was named by the Culinary Institute as
Outstanding Culinarian, a title won by only four people in the
last thirty years. The Bakery has also been a winner of *Holiday*
magazine's Dining Award for eight consecutive years. The specialties are consistently tasty and vary by season. Thirteen dollars is the price for a five-course dinner, with interesting selections such as the Beef Wellington, duck served with a cherry
sauce or roast pork with Hungarian sausage.

Pears Hélène

Serves 8

8 firm pears (d'Anjou or
   Wilhelm)
1 quart water
6 whole cloves
2" cinnamon stick
1 cup sugar
   Juice of 1 lemon

4 teaspoons tart jelly, such
   as red currant
8 small pieces spongecake,
   or any leftover cake
1 recipe Basic Vanilla
   Cream (see below)
1 recipe Chocolate Sauce
   (see below)

Peel pears, leaving stems on. Cut a slice from the bottom of each so that pears stand on flat surface. Remove core from bottom, leaving a hole big enough to turn a teaspoon in. Combine water, cloves, cinnamon stick, sugar and lemon juice; bring to a boil. Add pears to the liquid, boil again, then reduce heat to low. Simmer under cover until pears are fork tender, approximately 1 hour.

Remove pan from heat and cool until lukewarm. Remove pears with a slotted spoon. Place on tray and chill in refrigerator. When pears have chilled, stuff each with ½ teaspoon of jelly and a piece of cake. Place each pear in an individual glass dish with ½ cup of Basic Vanilla Cream. Spoon chocolate sauce over each and serve.

BASIC VANILLA CREAM

½ cup (8 tablespoons)
   cornstarch
1 quart milk
3 egg yolks

½ cup sugar
½ teaspoon salt
1 teaspoon vanilla
3 ounces butter

Dissolve cornstarch in 1 cup of the milk. Beat the egg yolks slightly with a fork and add to the cornstarch mixture. Place the remaining 3 cups milk in a saucepan. Add sugar, salt, vanilla and butter. Heat mixture, stirring to dissolve sugar. When mixture boils, stir with a wire whip and pour in the milk-cornstarch-egg mixture. Beat vigorously; it will become very stiff. It will not be necessary to cook more than 5 minutes, as it will thicken almost immediately. Remove from heat as soon as cream is smooth and thick. Let cool.

CHOCOLATE SAUCE

¼ cup unsalted butter
1 cup sugar
½ cup good quality cocoa
1 cup milk
1 tablespoon cornstarch
mixed with ¼ cup cold water
½ cup commercial chocolate syrup
¼ cup brandy

In a heavy saucepan, melt butter with the sugar and cocoa until mixture starts to caramelize. Immediately add the milk, stirring constantly. The hard lumps will dissolve as liquid comes to a boil. Pour the cornstarch mixture in a slow stream into boiling syrup, stirring constantly. Remove from fire and allow to cool to room temperature. Dilute with the chocolate syrup and brandy. Refrigerate. The sauce, refrigerated, can be kept up to two weeks. From the *Chef's Secret Cookbook*, published by Quadrangle, with the permission of the author.

THE BARN OF BARRINGTON

ADDRESS   1415 South Barrington Road, Barrington
TELEPHONE   381-8585
HOURS AND DAYS   Lunch: Tues.–Fri. and Sun. 11 A.M.–2:30
        P.M.
        Dinner: Tues.–Sat. 5–11 P.M.;
        Sun. 5–10 P.M.
HOLIDAYS CLOSED   Christmas, New Year's Day
RESERVATIONS   Yes
CREDIT CARDS   AE, MC, VI
ENTERTAINMENT   Pianist: Tues.–Sat. 6–11 P.M. in the Music
        Room
        Harpist: Sun. 6–10 P.M. in the Great Hall
PARKING   300 cars
BANQUET FACILITIES   From 20 to 250
DRESS   Jacket
LIQUOR   Yes
WINE   Extensive selection

The decor of the Barn is magnificent. Unlike the usual barn, the Barn's foyer has a huge fireplace and a winding stairway up to the Great Hall. The Great Hall is decorated with original paintings and eighteenth-century tapestries. Specialties are Coq au Vin Rouge, scampi, and veal steak with swiss cheese and ham. The food available in the Carvey Room includes steaks, seafood and flamed duckling. A good deal is available from 5 to 6:30 P.M., when a fixed-price dinner is eight dollars. The discotheque swings on Tues., Fri. and Sat. nights. Free dancing lessons for guests are given on Tues. nights from 8 to 10 P.M. It is a fun place no matter when you go.

Poulet au Curry

Serves 4

2½ -pound, frying chicken
½ teaspoon salt
3 tablespoons oil
1 medium onion, finely
  chopped
1 medium apple, peeled,
  cored and shredded

3 teaspoons curry powder
1 tablespoon flour
1½ cups chicken stock (from
  chicken skin and bones)
Juice of 1 large orange
¼ cup cream
2 tablespoons coconut milk

Cut chicken in 4 pieces, debone and remove skin. Make 1½ cups stock with skin and bones. Sprinkle chicken with salt. Sauté chicken pieces in oil without browning. Add onion and apple; stir. Add curry powder. As soon as chicken pieces are firm, sprinkle in flour. Stir ingredients while adding stock and orange juice, then cover and simmer for 10 minutes. Add cream and coconut milk; cook for 1 minute. Serve with cooked rice.
Wine suggestion: Dry white Burgundy or California wine

BENIHANA OF TOKYO

ADDRESS   166 East Superior Street
TELEPHONE   664-9643
HOURS AND DAYS   Lunch: Mon.–Sat. 11:30 A.M.–2 P.M.
       Dinner: Mon.–Thurs. 5:30–11 P.M.;
       Fri. 5:30 P.M.–midnight;
       Sat. 5 P.M.–midnight;
       Sun. 4–11 P.M.
HOLIDAYS CLOSED   Dinner only on all holidays
RESERVATIONS   Weekends only
CREDIT CARDS   All major cards
ENTERTAINMENT   Guitarist
PARKING   Yes
BANQUET FACILITIES   Up to 180
DRESS   Informal
LIQUOR   Yes
WINE   Limited selection
OTHER LOCATIONS: Route 22 and Milwaukee Ave., Lincolnshire

Your chef's kitchen is the grill in the center of your table. He cuts, seasons and cooks your meal with quick movements that seem so easy, while the rest of you fumble with your chopsticks. Our group enjoyed the Japanese Onion Soup, Hibachi Chicken and Sukiyaki Steak. If you object to being seated with strangers, bring along a group of six to guarantee your own table.

Ginger Sauce

Serves 6

½ cup soy sauce
¼ cup vinegar
1 small sliced onion
1 small piece fresh ginger
   root (if not available,

substitute ⅛ teaspoon
powdered ginger)
Pinch of MSG
(monosodium glutamate)

Place all ingredients in an electric blender and set at high speed. Mix for two minutes or until ginger and onions are finely chopped. Ginger Sauce is used as a dip for cooked shrimp or vegetables.

BERGHOFF RESTAURANT

ADDRESS   17 West Adams Street
TELEPHONE   427-3170
HOURS AND DAYS   Mon.–Sat. 11 A.M.–9:30 P.M.
HOLIDAYS CLOSED   All major holidays
RESERVATIONS   No
CREDIT CARDS   No
ENTERTAINMENT   No
PARKING   After 3:30 P.M., at 17 East Adams: $1.25 plus tax
BANQUET FACILITIES   Yes
DRESS   Informal
LIQUOR   Yes
WINE   Limited list

This restaurant was founded in 1898. It is one of the most consistently good restaurants in the city. When you sit down, you are given fresh rye bread and butter to munch on. The oak-paneled rooms and the waiters running around, working efficiently, give you the feeling that you are in Germany. They have their own specially brewed Muenchner-style beer and their own sour mash Kentucky bourbons. They feature seasonal dishes such as hasenpfeffer, roast venison, cornish hen at Christmas and special fish dishes during Lent. The wienerschnitzel, fresh seafood and aged steaks are all carefully prepared. The strawberry shortcake is a good dessert to keep in mind.

Gschnaetzlets (Veal Ragout)

Serves 5

2½ pounds veal sliced in 2"
  strips
¼ pound butter
 4 ounces fresh mushrooms,
  sliced fine
½ pound onions, sliced fine

1½ cups brown gravy (your
  favorite)
3 ounces (6 tablespoons)
  white wine
  Salt to taste
3 dashes Tabasco Sauce
4 ounces (¼ cup) sour cream

Brown the veal in the butter; remove from pan. Sauté onions
and mushrooms in remaining butter, and return meat to pan.
Add the gravy and wine and cook for 20 minutes. Season with
salt and Tabasco Sauce. Remove from heat and stir in the sour
cream.

Wine suggestion: Medium white German wine

BEVERLY HOUSE

ADDRESS   10247 South Beverly Avenue
TELEPHONE   238-2105
HOURS AND DAYS   Mon.–Thurs. 11 A.M.–10 P.M.;
      Fri., Sat. 11 A.M.–midnight;
      Sun. 11 A.M.–9 P.M.
HOLIDAYS CLOSED   Memorial Day, July 4, Labor Day
RESERVATIONS   Not necessary
CREDIT CARDS   AE, DC
ENTERTAINMENT   Strolling musicians in fall and winter
PARKING   Yes
BANQUET FACILITIES   Yes
DRESS   Casual
LIQUOR   Yes
WINE   Limited wine list

This neighborhood restaurant, serving French and American cuisine, has won many impressive awards. It has received the *Holiday* Award, the Food and Wine Society Award and the Gold Escoffier Medal—the highest honor given by the Chef de Cuisine Association. Their internationally known chef, Mr. Corkald, advanced from assistant chef on an Adriatic Sealiner to chef at renowned hotels throughout the United States. The menu is varied. We had a delicious Long Island Duckling with Bing cherries and wild rice and the Veal Cordon Bleu. You can also order a simple grilled cheese or bacon, lettuce and tomato sandwich.

Beef Wellington

Serves 2

16-ounce beef tenderloin,
   trimmed
   Salt and pepper
1 small clove garlic, crushed
2 shallots
2 tablespoons oil
10 fresh, finely chopped
   mushrooms

1 ounce dry red wine
½ cup brown gravy
4 ounces foie gras or chicken
   liver pâté
1 egg yolk
1 recipe Pastry Dough (see
   below)
2 eggs

Season tenderloin with salt and pepper to taste and sear in a very hot pan. Remove and let cool. In a separate pan, sauté garlic and shallots in oil and add the mushrooms. Add the red wine and reduce; add brown gravy and reduce further until you have a very heavy purée. Mash pâté and add to above mixture with egg yolk and salt and pepper to taste. Coat the cooled steak with this mixture. Place steak on dough which has been rolled out to a thickness of ¼″, reserving enough for decoration. Wrap dough around steak, and completely seal the seam on the bottom. Decorate top with reserved dough in lattice work or any suitable design. Beat the two eggs and use to brush dough. Bake in 375° oven for ½ hour or until golden brown. Slice and serve with either a bordelaise or béarnaise sauce on the side.

PASTRY DOUGH

2 cups flour
4 tablespoons unsalted
   butter

4 tablespoons shortening
2 egg yolks
3 tablespoons ice water

In a small mixing bowl, combine the flour, butter and shortening. Rub the flour and butter together with your fingers until the mixture resembles a coarse meal. Add the egg yolks and combine thoroughly. Pour the ice water over the mixture, knead and gather the dough into one ball. If the dough crumbles, add more ice water, a small amount at a time, until dough is workable. Dust the dough with flour, wrap in wax paper and refrigerate for at least 1 hour. Roll on floured surface.

Wine suggestion: Dry red Burgundy, Bordeaux or California wine

THE BIRD

ADDRESS   5001 West Dempster Street, Skokie
TELEPHONE   679-5855
HOURS AND DAYS   Thurs.–Fri. 6:30–9:30 P.M.; Sat. 6–9:30 P.M.;
      Sun. 5–8:30 P.M.
HOLIDAYS CLOSED   All holidays
RESERVATIONS   A must
CREDIT CARDS   No
ENTERTAINMENT   No
PARKING   Yes
BANQUET FACILITIES   Yes
DRESS   Casual
LIQUOR   No
WINE   No, bring your own

Taking a ride on the Skokie Swift? No—it's actually a unique Cantonese restaurant called The Bird, hidden in the rear of this CTA-station converted coffee shop. All the meals are set-price and consist of six courses which Mrs. Moy, your gracious hostess, will tell you about at tableside. Mr. Moy is in the kitchen preparing your dinner from the fresh produce he has bought at the market that morning. The gourmet offering could begin with crispy chicken wings stuffed with shrimp or chicken livers, and continue with Peking Duck, beef and tomatoes, shrimp in the shells soaked in light soy sauce, and Lemon Chicken. If you are lucky the last course might be the fresh fish of the day, cooked Cantonese style, and filleted at your table. Bring your own wine and a big appetite.

Drunken Mermaids (Shrimp)

Serves 4

4–6 tablespoons peanut oil
   Several drops sesame oil
  1 teaspoon salt
1½ pounds Louisiana white
   shrimp in shell

2–3 tablespoons chopped green
  onion
1 tablespoon chopped fresh
  ginger root
⅓ cup light soy sauce
⅓ cup dry white wine

Heat peanut and sesame oils and salt in skillet over high heat. (Salt prevents oil from catching fire.) Cook shrimp rapidly. Cover for one minute. Remove cover and add green onion and ginger. Stir quickly to blend. Add soy sauce and wine. Mix well. Serve immediately with shrimp still in shell.

Drink suggestion: Saki, hot or chilled (not tepid)

THE BLACKHAWK

ADDRESS   139 North Wabash Avenue
TELEPHONE   726-0100
HOURS AND DAYS   Mon.–Fri. 11 A.M.–10:30 P.M.; Sat. 11 A.M.–
    11 P.M.; Sun. 3:30–10:30 P.M.
HOLIDAYS CLOSED   All major holidays
RESERVATIONS   Preferred
CREDIT CARDS   AE, CB, DC, MC, VI
ENTERTAINMENT   No
PARKING $1.00 parking after 5 P.M. for dinner guests (exc. Sun.)
BANQUET FACILITIES   From 50 to 250
DRESS   Casual
LIQUOR   Yes
WINE   Good selection
OTHER LOCATION   110 East Pearson (943-3300)

This restaurant has been famous since 1920. It's as popular today as it was then. The food is of very high quality. The spinning salad bowl is famous and Blackhawk Salad Dressing is bottled and available in most Chicagoland supermarkets. The specialties include Roast Prime Rib of Beef, broiled steaks and fresh Boston scrod. The Blackhawk at 110 East Pearson is also a good place to dine near the Magnificent Mile (Michigan Avenue).

Blackhawk Salad

Serves 4–6

1 package (3 ounces) cream cheese, softened
3 ounces blue cheese, crumbled
5–6 tablespoons water
1 egg
1 tablespoon plus 1½ teaspoons lemon juice
1 cup vegetable oil
¼ cup red wine vinegar
¼ teaspoon sharp prepared mustard
¾ teaspoon paprika
¾ teaspoon salt
¼ teaspoon garlic powder
¼ teaspoon white pepper
1 tablespoon sugar
2 tablespoons snipped chives
1½ teaspoons Worcestershire sauce
2 tablespoons salad-and-sandwich sauce
8 cups bite-size pieces salad greens (Bibb, iceberg, endive)
Seasoned salt
1 hard-cooked egg, chopped
Freshly ground pepper
8 anchovy fillets

Beat cheeses until smooth. Beat in water, 1 tablespoon at a time, until mixture is of pouring consistency; reserve. Place egg, lemon juice and ¼ cup of the oil in blender container; cover. Blend on medium speed 15 seconds. Increase to high speed; add remaining oil very slowly. Turn off blender occasionally and clean sides of container with rubber spatula. Add vinegar, mustard, seasonings, sugar, chives, Worcestershire sauce and salad sauce to blender container; cover. Blend on high speed until smooth. Place salad greens in bowl. Pour enough dressing over greens to coat. Sprinkle salad with seasoned salt and chopped egg. Toss gently 3 times. Sprinkle with pepper. Add 2 to 3 tablespoons reserved cheese mixture. Toss gently 3 times. Garnish with anchovies. (Tip: Remaining dressing and cheese mixture can be stored covered in refrigerator up to 2 weeks.)

LE BON VIVANT

ADDRESS   222 Greenwood Avenue, Glenview
TELEPHONE   967-1222
HOURS AND DAYS   Lunch: Tues.–Fri. 11:30 A.M.–2:30 P.M.
        Dinner: Tues.–Thurs. 5–10 P.M.; Fri., Sat. 5–11:30 P.M.
HOLIDAYS CLOSED   Christmas, New Year's Day
RESERVATIONS   Yes
CREDIT CARDS   MC, VI
ENTERTAINMENT   No
PARKING   By attendant
BANQUET FACILITIES   Private parties, up to 80
DRESS   Jacket required
LIQUOR   Yes
WINE   Good selection

There is an air of regal splendor when you enter this restaurant. You'll see fresh flowers, white tablecloths, delicate china and pretty silver pieces. There is no definite bar; however, as you are waiting for your table you can get a drink in the quaint, gracious lobby. The seafood crepe, veal scallops, poached salmon and beef tournedos are all marvelous. For dessert try the baked alaska, chocolate mousse or caramel custard. This is an exceptional restaurant, to which you will be anxious to return.

Fruits de Mer

Serves 4

4 ounces (¼ cup) olive oil
8 ounces lobster tail meat
8 fresh shrimp, shelled,
    deveined and butterflied
6 ounces Alaskan king
    crabmeat
4 ounces fresh sliced
    mushrooms
2 ounces (¼ cup) sliced
    green pepper
1 large garlic clove, chopped
    very fine

1 ounce (2 tablespoons) dry
    sherry wine
Salt and pepper to taste
¼ teaspoon MSG
    (monosodium glutamate)
¼ ounce (1½ teaspoons)
    fresh lemon juice
1 teaspoon parsley, chopped
4 artichoke hearts, cut in
    half
8 pimiento-stuffed green
    olives, cut in half

Heat a 10″ pan over high heat. Add olive oil, then add lobster, shrimp, crabmeat, mushrooms, green peppers, and garlic. Toss lightly with wooden spoon for 1 minute on high heat. Flame with sherry. Season with salt, pepper, and MSG. Cover and cook for 2 minutes. Add lemon juice, parsley, artichoke hearts and olives. Toss lightly again. Cover and simmer for 2 minutes. Serve with your favorite rice pilaf.

Wine suggestion: Medium white Portuguese wine

THE BRASSARY

ADDRESS   625 North Michigan Avenue
TELEPHONE   266-2757
HOURS AND DAYS   Mon.–Fri. 11 A.M.–midnight; Sat., Sun. 11
    A.M.–5 P.M.
HOLIDAYS CLOSED   Memorial Day, July 4, Thanksgiving,
    Christmas, New Year's Day
RESERVATIONS   Advisable for lunch only
CREDIT CARDS   AE
ENTERTAINMENT   No
PARKING   No
BANQUET FACILITIES   Sat. and Sun. evenings
DRESS   Casual
LIQUOR   Yes
WINE   Limited selection

If you are on Michigan Avenue and looking for a casual, colorful, fun-loving restaurant, this is a darling little find. It is known for its super hamburgers, onion rings, minestrone soup and Scutzafarno Pizza Sausage Sandwich. A fresh salad bar with all the necessary trimmings is available. It is a singles spot and at times very lively with throngs of people. There are outdoor tables during the summer months. Service is friendly and attentive.

Scutzafarno Pizza Sausage Sandwich

Serves 8

2 *pounds pizza sausage*
1 *teaspoon salt*
1 *teaspoon pepper*
1 *teaspoon oregano*
8 *kaiser rolls*

4 *green peppers*
2 *tablespoons oil*
½ *pound mozzarella cheese*
18-*ounce can pizza sauce*

Mix pizza sausage, salt, pepper and oregano together. Shape into 8 quarter-pound patties. Place on baking sheet in 325° oven for approximately 25 minutes. While sausage is cooking, cut green peppers into strips; sauté in oil until tender. Slice kaiser rolls in half. Remove sausage from oven; place 1 ounce mozzarella on each sausage patty and return to oven until cheese melts. Place each patty on the bottom half of a kaiser roll; top with pepper strips and pizza sauce. Put top of roll on and serve while hot.

Wine suggestion: Dry red Italian wine

BROWN BEAR RESTAURANT

ADDRESS   6318 North Clark Street
TELEPHONE   274-1200
HOURS AND DAYS   Tues.–Sat. 11 A.M.–midnight; Sun. 1–11 P.M.
Bar hours Tues.–Fri. 11 A.M.–2 A.M.; Sat. 11 A.M.–3
A.M.; Sun. 1 P.M.–midnight
HOLIDAYS CLOSED   Only if they fall on a Monday
RESERVATIONS   Suggested
CREDIT CARDS   All major credit cards
ENTERTAINMENT   Yes
PARKING   Yes
BANQUET FACILITIES   Up to 150
DRESS   Casual
LIQUOR   Yes
WINE   Limited selection

This restaurant provides a very cheerful and friendly dining atmosphere. The accent is on robust German cooking—sauerbraten, Wiener Schnitzel a la Holstein, and smoked pork loin. The food is well prepared and the portions generous. The varied entertainment manages to get your feet moving and your hands clapping. There are a lot of funny songs and lively dances, which create a joyous atmosphere. Be sure to call in advance if there is a birthday or anniversary, because they provide a piece of pastry and sparkler. Service is always good.

Sauerbraten

Serves 4

2 quarts water
2 quarts cider vinegar
1 tablespoon powdered
  allspice
1 teaspoon salt
1 large onion, sliced
2 carrots, sliced

4 pounds trimmed round of
  beef
1 cup flour
½ cup sour cream
1 cup (8 ounces) Burgundy
  wine

To make marinade: Combine water, vinegar, allspice, salt, onion, and carrot. Bring ingredients to a boil and let cool. Pour marinade over beef and let stand in refrigerator, uncovered, 3 to 4 days. *For preparation of entree:* Take beef out of marinade and brown in oven at 350°. Add flour and 2 cups of marinade and bake about 2 hours longer. Strain gravy; stir in sour cream and Burgundy. Slice beef; pour gravy over meat. Great served with potato pancakes or dumplings and red cabbage.
Wine suggestion: Full-bodied white German wine

CAFÉ ÁZTECA

ADDRESS   215 West North Avenue
TELEPHONE   944-9854
HOURS AND DAYS   Daily noon–1 A.M.
HOLIDAYS CLOSED   Thanksgiving, Christmas, New Year's Day
RESERVATIONS   Weekends only
CREDIT CARDS   AE, CB, DC
ENTERTAINMENT   Yes
PARKING   No
BANQUET FACILITIES   Private parties up to 100
DRESS   Casual
LIQUOR   Yes
WINE   Limited selection

Cafe Ázteca is one of the oldest Mexican restaurants in Chicago. It has a beautiful outdoor garden for summer dining, with peach, pear, cherry and apple trees, a grape arbor and fresh flowers. The delightful year-round entertainment consists of authentic Mexican singing, guitars and an unusual Mexican harp. The menu includes Mexican as well as outstanding Spanish specialties. The Enchiladas Federico are great. They are chicken-filled and covered with a rich wine and mushroom sauce. Treat yourself to a little of everything and order the Combinacion Ázteca. This choice includes taco, Enchilada Ázteca, and Tostada. It makes an exceptional meal.

Kamoosh Appetizer

Serves 4

4 corn tortillas
Oil for frying
¾ cup refried beans
(available at ethnic food
stores)

¾ cup tomato sauce
1 cup grated cheddar cheese
Guacamole (homemade,
canned or frozen)

Quarter tortillas and deep-fry. Spread a thin layer of refried beans on each quarter and arrange, in a single layer, on an oven-proof dish. Pour tomato sauce over all bean-covered chips. Sprinkle with grated cheese and place in broiler until cheese is melted. Garnish top of each chip with about 1 teaspoon of guacamole. Serve hot. Allow 4 quarters per person.

Drink suggestion: Carta Blanca or Dos Equis beer

CAFE BOHEMIA

ADDRESS   138 South Clinton Street
TELEPHONE   782-1826
HOURS AND DAYS   Mon.–Sat. 11:30 A.M.–midnight
HOLIDAYS CLOSED   All major holidays
RESERVATIONS   Not needed
CREDIT CARDS   CB, DC, MC, VI
ENTERTAINMENT   No
PARKING   Doorman
BANQUET FACILITIES   Yes
DRESS   Informal
LIQUOR   Yes
WINE   Good selection

Cafe Bohemia is a family-owned restaurant that has been in business for 60 years. They are famous for their unique and extensive selection of superbly prepared wild game dishes such as moose, buffalo and African lion steak. Try the venison steak served with wild rice. For the not-so-daring patron, the largest selection in town of steaks, fowl and seafood is available. Also among our favorites are the whole Maine lobster—a real treat—and the extra-crisp roast duck served with wild rice. The price of your entree includes appetizer, soup, salad, a vegetable dish, potato or their excellent dumplings, dessert and coffee. Lighter meals are available and are served at a la carte prices.

Roast Duck

Serves 3–4

1 4½ to 5½-pound ready-to-cook duck
Salt and white pepper

MSG (monosodium glutamate)
Caraway seeds
2 tablespoons flour

Wash duck and set aside the giblets. Sprinkle with salt, white pepper and MSG. Then sprinkle lightly with caraway seeds, inside and out. Roast, uncovered, at 400° until brown. Turn and reduce heat to 350° and cook for 1½ hours or until duck is tender. Simmer giblets in water to cover until tender. Reserve cooking liquid; chop giblets fine. Make a roux of about 2 tablespoons of duck drippings and the flour. Add giblets and liquid. Simmer until of desired thickness. Serve with wild rice or dumplings.

Wine suggestion: Medium red Rhône wine

CAFÉ METROPOLE

ADDRESS   2828 North Clark Street
TELEPHONE   935-6600
HOURS AND DAYS   Daily 11:30 A.M.–midnight
HOLIDAYS CLOSED   Christmas, New Year's Day
RESERVATIONS   No
CREDIT CARDS   No
ENTERTAINMENT   Yes, after 9 P.M.: Piano player and violinist
PARKING   Attached garage
BANQUET FACILITIES   No
DRESS   Casual
LIQUOR   Yes
WINE   Limited selection

The location of Café Metropole is quite unusual, but proves to be very exciting. It is set in the center atrium court of the Century Shopping Center, which creates the feeling of outdoor dining all year round. The 6 surrounding circular levels of shops and shoppers offer the sport of people-watching to the diners. Once you've tried the onion soup or gazpacho, you'll never forget them. They are both truly outstanding. The sandwiches consist of tasty meat and cheese or tomato combinations held together by a toasted bun. You can't possibly go wrong with any item you choose to order here.

Salade Niçoise

Serves 6

4 tomatoes, quartered	8 ripe olives
½ large bermuda onion, sliced into rings	8 anchovy filets
	2 hard-boiled eggs, quartered
1 sweet bell pepper, sliced into rings	1 can tuna fish, or sliced breast of turkey, or try smoked oysters
2 medium heads of romaine lettuce, chopped and dried	Salad Dressing (see below
3 stalks of celery, sliced	

Toss prepared vegetables in salad bowl, then place the garniture (olives, anchovies, eggs, meat) neatly on top. Sprinkle with salad dressing and serve.

SALAD DRESSING

½ teaspoon kosher salt	¼ teaspoon pepper
2 cloves garlic	¼ teaspoon basil
½ cup wine vinegar	¼ teaspoon oregano
Dash lemon juice	¼ teaspoon sugar
Dash Worcestershire sauce	¼ teaspoon tarragon
½ teaspoon dry mustard	½ cup olive oil

Put salt in wooden bowl, to aid in grinding garlic. Crush garlic first with fork, then with back of spoon until it liquefies. Add all liquid ingredients but oil; add seasonings and whip with hand whisk. Blend in olive oil slowly until completely bound.

Wine suggestion: Provençale dry rosé

CAMELLIA HOUSE AND TERRACE LOUNGE

ADDRESS   140 East Walton Street (The Drake Hotel)
TELEPHONE   787-2200
HOURS AND DAYS   Tues.–Sat. 5 P.M.–2 A.M.; Sun. brunch
noon–4 P.M.
HOLIDAYS CLOSED   New Year's Day
RESERVATIONS   Suggested
CREDIT CARDS   AE, Drake Credit Card
ENTERTAINMENT   Live—continuous music and dancing—show
times 8:30 P.M., 11 P.M.
PARKING   Valet parking
BANQUET FACILITIES   Small parties accepted
DRESS   Jacket
LIQUOR   Yes
WINE   Limited selection

The Camellia House and Terrace Lounge features continuous entertainment and dancing and serves Continental foods. Specialties are Lobster Thermidor, Roast Duckling Bigarade (orange sauce), and Escalopine of Veal Marsala. The drinks, food and entertainment found here make it a special place for a fun evening out on the town. The dim lights sparkle through crystal chandeliers and the lovely table settings provide an intimate environment.

Roast Wisconsin Duckling, Bigarade Sauce

Serves 4

2 5-pound Wisconsin
   ducklings
2 cups brown sugar, firmly
   packed

4 ounces (½ cup) orange
   juice
2 ounces (¼ cup) currant
   jelly
6 sections orange

Roast whole ducklings for 1½ hours at 375°. Cut ducklings in half and debone. To pan drippings add brown sugar, orange juice and jelly and cook for five minutes. Garnish with orange sections.

Wine suggestion: Medium red Rhône wine

CANDLELIGHT DINNER PLAYHOUSE

ADDRESS   5620 South Harlem Avenue, Summit
TELEPHONE   458-7373
HOURS AND DAYS   Tues.–Fri. 6 P.M.;
            Sat. 4 P.M. and 9 P.M.;
            Sun. 12:30 P.M. and 5:30 P.M.
            Curtain time is 2 hours after dinner
HOLIDAYS CLOSED   None
RESERVATIONS   Yes
CREDIT CARDS   AE, MC
ENTERTAINMENT   Professional stage productions
PARKING   Yes, free
BANQUET FACILITIES   Up to 585 people
DRESS   Semi-casual to semi-formal
LIQUOR   Yes
WINE   Limited selection

Candlelight is Chicago's original dinner playhouse. The only lights you see, upon entering, are the flickering candles set on each table. This aids in creating an intimate atmosphere in a room that seats 600 people. After dining, you remain in your seat to view the theater production. The tables are arranged on various levels for good viewing. You can certainly be assured of a well-priced, delightful evening of good food and exciting theater. The prices of the theater-dinner combinations vary according to the day. Weekdays it's $8.95 per person. On Friday and Sunday nights the price is $9.95 and Saturday night it's $10.95 per person. The menu gives you a selection of four entrees and includes a salad, Italian bread, a vegetable, potato and coffee. Your choice usually consists of roast sirloin of beef, baked mostaccioli and meatball, roast chicken or baked Boston scrod, served with a lemon-butter sauce. Other entrees are available at an additional cost.

Pork in Wine Sauce

Serves 4

1 *medium onion*	*Thyme*
1 *green pepper*	*Salt and pepper to taste*
1 *clove garlic*	1 *can condensed cream of*
4 *tablespoons margarine*	*mushroom soup*
6 *pork chops*	¼ *cup red wine*
Oregano	½ *cup light cream*

In a saucepan, brown onion, green pepper and garlic in margarine. Add pork chops seasoned with oregano, thyme, salt and pepper. Add mushroom soup and wine. Simmer for 40 minutes. Remove pork chops and cut from bone. Return meat to pan. Add cream and simmer for 5 minutes. Serve over wild rice.
Wine suggestion: Medium white California wine

CANTONESE CAFE

ADDRESS   937 North Rush Street
TELEPHONE   337-1248
HOURS AND DAYS   Mon.–Fri. 11:30 A.M.–10 P.M.;
        Sat. 11:30 A.M.–11 P.M.;
        Sun. 2–10 P.M.
HOLIDAYS CLOSED   Thanksgiving, Christmas
RESERVATIONS   Yes
CREDIT CARDS   No
ENTERTAINMENT   No
PARKING   No
BANQUET FACILITIES   No
DRESS   Casual
LIQUOR   Yes
WINE   Small selection of house wines

This restaurant has been operating on Rush Street for over 40 years, making it the oldest Chinese dining spot in the area. The menu offers first, an extensive selection of Cantonese dishes; second, their unique gourmet ideas; and third, American suggestions. The sweet and sour selections are fantastic and made with a tasty, succulent sauce. The Pork Egg Foo Young is another favorite. There's also a nice list of tropical drinks available. If you enjoy a beef dish, try the Steak Kow—beef tenderloin slices combined with Chinese greens, pea pods, water chestnuts, bamboo shoots and slices of black mushrooms. If you live in the area, call them for a delivery. It's a special treat that we rely on heavily.

Phoenix Shrimp

Serves 2

16 *large shrimp*
¼ *cup peanut oil*
4 *strips bacon, each cut in 4 pieces*
Batter (see below)

1 *heart of lettuce, shredded*
Sweet and Sour Sauce (see below)
¼ *cup almonds, chopped fine*

Shell and devein the shrimp. Cut almost through lengthwise (butterfly style) and flatten out each shrimp. Dry with paper towel. Heat the peanut oil in a frying pan. When fairly hot, place one piece of bacon over one shrimp. Dip into batter and place in frying pan. Cook and turn until both sides are golden brown. When finished, place the shrimp on top of shredded lettuce. Heat the sweet and sour sauce and pour over the shrimp. Sprinkle chopped almonds on top.

BATTER

4 *tablespoons flour*
2 *eggs, lightly beaten*
½ *teaspoon thin (light) soy sauce*

Pinch of white pepper
½ *teaspoon cooking sherry*
1 *green onion, chopped fine*

Combine all ingredients and beat until smooth.

SAUCE

½ *cup sugar*
½ *cup vinegar*
¼ *cup pineapple juice*
4 *tablespoons tomato catsup*
1 *teaspoon salt*

¼ *teaspoon Tabasco Sauce*
2½ *teaspoons cornstarch dissolved in ½ cup of water*

Place all ingredients for sauce, except cornstarch mixture, in a heavy saucepan. Bring to a boil; stir in the cornstarch mixture to thicken.
Wine suggestion: Dry white Loire wine

CAPE COD ROOM

ADDRESS   140 East Walton Street (The Drake Hotel)
TELEPHONE   787-2200
HOURS AND DAYS   Daily noon–midnight
HOLIDAYS CLOSED   Christmas
RESERVATIONS   Required
CREDIT CARDS   AE, Drake Credit Card
ENTERTAINMENT   No
PARKING   Valet service parking
BANQUET FACILITIES   No
DRESS   Jacket
LIQUOR   Yes
WINE   Good selection

The Cape Cod Room, a *Holiday* Restaurant Award winner for 22 consecutive years, features the choice catches of lakes, streams, and oceans—fresh and flavorful each day—served in the atmosphere of East Boston. You can depend on the food here to be outstanding. You will especially enjoy eating the Bookbinder Soup (red snapper with sherry), the shoestring potatoes, the Pompano Papillote (with lobster and mushrooms), the turbot, lobster, scallops, Filet of Lemon Sole Amandine, Colorado rainbow trout, lake perch, and, for dessert, the Frozen Chocolate Ice Cream Pie.

Pompano Papillote à la Drake

Serves 6

½ teaspoon chopped shallots
½ cup sliced mushrooms
½ cup diced cooked lobster
  meat
½ teaspoon Worcestershire
  sauce
½ teaspoon salt
 2 tablespoons butter

6 filets of pompano, 7
  ounces each
6 ounces (¾ cup) red wine
6 ounces (¾ cup) water
  Parchment paper for
  baking
  Oil

Sauté shallots, mushrooms, lobster, Worcestershire sauce and salt in butter for 5 minutes. Place pompano filets evenly in pan; add wine and water and poach for 20 minutes. From parchment paper cut 6 large heart shapes, each 22″ wide and 14″ long. Place individual paper hearts on working table; brush lightly with cooking oil. On the left section of each paper place one fish filet. Cover with ⅙ of sauce from pan. Fold the right side of paper heart over the filet, turning all edges to form a tight seal, thus preventing air from escaping the bag. Preheat oven to 350°. Place individual bags, sealed edge down, on baking sheet; heat in oven until each bag begins to puff up. Serve on a china platter, allowing each guest to open his or her own bag.
Wine suggestion: Medium white German wine

CASBAH II

ADDRESS   514 Diversey Avenue
TELEPHONE   935-7570
HOURS AND DAYS   Daily 5–11 P.M.
HOLIDAYS CLOSED   Thanksgiving, Christmas
RESERVATIONS   Suggested
CREDIT CARDS   CB, DC, MC, VI
ENTERTAINMENT   No
PARKING   Free at Rienzie Garage, ½ block west
BANQUET FACILITIES   No
DRESS   Casual
LIQUOR   Yes
WINE   Limited selection

Year after year, this Armenian restaurant has been given 4 stars by the Mobil Guide and has received high praise from the food critics. The Middle Eastern entrees consist of interesting combinations of lamb, beef and vegetables, all served with fresh pita bread. Maglube—spiced rice cooked with lamb, cauliflower and pine nuts—is certainly worth trying; however, it's available on weekends only. The Armenian Kabab is a delicious combination of tastes. It includes cubes of beef, green peppers, onions, tomatoes and eggplant. For an interesting first course, try the Plaki—white beans, carrots, garlic and parsley with lemon juice. All dinners include Hommos or Djadjic, egg-lemon soup and a tossed salad.

Maglube

Serves 4

1 head of cauliflower
1 cup vegetable shortening
2½ pounds meat from leg of
lamb
1 large onion

Salt, cinnamon and
cloves, to taste
2 cups rice (soak rice in hot
water for 15 minutes)
Pine nuts, sautéed in
vegetable shortening

Boil cauliflower in water to cover for 3 minutes. Break into flowerets. Fry in hot shortening until golden brown. Drain on absorbent paper. Cover meat with water and boil with onion, salt, cinnamon and cloves until tender. Drain broth into bowl. Put the cauliflower, meat and rice in layers in a 4-quart pot. Add reserved broth to cover rice; if not enough broth, add plain water. Let this mixture come to a boil. Lower the heat and let it simmer until rice is tender and excess water is evaporated. Turn the pot upside down onto a platter and garnish with sautéed pine nuts.

Wine suggestion: Dry white Burgundy or dark or light beer

CHEF ALBERTO'S

ADDRESS   3200 North Lake Shore Drive
TELEPHONE   549-2515
HOURS AND DAYS   Tues.–Sun. 5–midnight
HOLIDAYS CLOSED   Christmas
RESERVATIONS   Suggested
CREDIT CARDS   AE, DC, MC
ENTERTAINMENT   No
PARKING   Inside, Belmont entrance
BANQUET FACILITIES   Up to 125 people
DRESS   Casual
LIQUOR   Yes
WINE   Good selection

Chef Alberto's is a charming restaurant overlooking Belmont Harbor. It offers an extensive selection of Continental specialties, including Chicken Kiev, Strip Steak alla Siciliana and roast duckling with the chef's own orange sauce. Also offered is fresh seafood, which is flown in daily. An excellent Caesar Salad and Fettucine Alfredo are served with all dinners.

Veal Picante

Serves 3

1 pound thin veal
   tenderloin
Flour
¼ cup olive oil
1 garlic clove
½ pound fresh sliced
   mushrooms

1½ ounces (3 tablespoons)
   lemon juice
1½ ounces (3 tablespoons) dry
   white wine
Capers (optional)
Lemon slices

Cut veal in small pieces (3″–4″). Pound the veal very thin and dust with flour. Sauté in skillet with olive oil and garlic; brown very lightly on both sides. Add mushrooms. Cook on high heat for 3 minutes. Add lemon juice and wine. Cook 3 more minutes, then add capers. Serve with lemon slices.

Wine suggestion: Dry white Italian wine

LA CHEMINÉE

ADDRESS   1161 North Dearborn Street
TELEPHONE   642-6654
HOURS AND DAYS   Lunch: Mon.–Fri. 11:30 A.M.–2:30 P.M.
        Dinner: Mon.–Sat. 5:30–10:30 P.M.
HOLIDAYS CLOSED   All national holidays
RESERVATIONS   Yes
CREDIT CARDS   AE, CB, DC, MC, VI
ENTERTAINMENT   No
PARKING   Reduced rate parking ½ block away
BANQUET FACILITIES   Up to 45
DRESS   Informal
LIQUOR   Yes
WINE   Extensive selection

La Cheminée is an authentic countryside French restaurant located in an old brownstone. The dimly lit and rustic atmosphere provides an intimate and charming spot to dine. It is a *Holiday* Award restaurant and rightly so. The extensive menu offers a variety of consistently good food. The hot seafood casserole is an enjoyable beginning to your meal. The Veal Florentine and the trout stuffed with seafood mousse are superb. End the meal with a selection from their fabulous, tempting desserts, such as Caramel Custard or Peach Melba. The price is set at $13.50 per person and includes an appetizer or soup, salad, entree, dessert and coffee.

Poulet Florentine

Serves 4

2 pounds fresh spinach or
three 10-ounce packages
frozen chopped spinach
3 quarts salted water,
boiling
6 ounces (1½ sticks) butter
12 ounces (1½ cups) heavy
cream

6 boned chicken breasts
1 tablespoon chopped
shallots
Salt and pepper
1 pint dry white wine
3 ounces (6 tablespoons)
flour

Cook fresh spinach about 3 minutes in boiling water. Drain and squeeze to extract as much water as possible, then chop. If using frozen spinach, follow package instructions for cooking and then drain. Melt 2 ounces (½ stick) of the butter in a small pot, add spinach and 4 ounces (½ cup) of the cream. Boil a few minutes, stirring, until there is no liquid left. Transfer spinach to a shallow baking dish, spread evenly and set aside.

Place chicken breasts in a skillet, sprinkle with chopped shallots and salt and pepper to taste, and pour in wine, which should cover chicken. Bring to a boil and let simmer gently for 10 minutes. Remove chicken, drain and fit snugly over spinach. Strain cooking liquid into a bowl and reserve for the sauce.

Melt the remaining butter in a small pan, add flour, mix evenly and cook slowly for 15 minutes, stirring frequently. Add cooking liquid of chicken, little by little, while whisking vigorously to avoid the formation of lumps. The sauce should be thick but smooth; if it is lumpy, strain through a sieve or fine strainer, then return to pan. Add remaining cream. Boil a few minutes while stirring until the sauce has a smooth, creamy consistency. Pour the sauce over the chicken and spinach to cover evenly and place dish under hot broiler until the sauce is golden.
Wine suggestion: Dry white Italian wine

CHEZ PAUL

ADDRESS   660 North Rush Street
TELEPHONE   944-6680
HOURS AND DAYS   Mon.–Fri. noon–10 P.M.;
        Sat. 5:30–11 P.M.;
        Sun. 5:30–10 P.M.
HOLIDAYS CLOSED   Easter, July 4, Labor Day, Christmas
RESERVATIONS   Yes
CREDIT CARDS   All major cards
ENTERTAINMENT   No
PARKING   Valet parking
BANQUET FACILITIES   Yes
DRESS   Jacket and tie
LIQUOR   Yes
WINE   Extensive selection

The exquisite mansion originally built for R. Hall McCormick, in 1875, is now the home of Chez Paul. Historical fixtures are found throughout the stately, yet warm decor. The French cuisine is consistently exceptional, which is why it has always been one of our favorites. The lamb chops are great, but our personal favorite is the duck, extra crisp, with the special fruit sauce. The desserts are tempting and fantastic, especially the Profiteroles au Chocolat. Service has always been perfect, which makes the total experience even more enjoyable. All items are a la carte.

Filet of Sole Chez Paul

Serves 4

14 tablespoons (1¾ sticks)
    butter
16 filets of Dover sole
2 ounces (¼ cup) chopped
    shallots
4 mushrooms

10 ounces (1¼ cups) white
    wine
1 pint fish stock
    Salt and pepper
½ pint heavy cream
    Lobster Butter (see below)

Melt 2 tablespoons butter in frying pan. Add sole, shallots, mushrooms, wine and fish stock and cook over medium heat for 2 minutes. Season with salt and pepper to taste. Place the filets on a platter and keep them warm. Reduce the fumet (broth) until almost dry and add cream; reduce again by ¾. Add remaining 12 tablespoons (1½ sticks) butter. Pass the lobster butter through a sieve or strainer onto the filets. Serve with rice or boiled potato.

LOBSTER BUTTER

Pound the creamy parts, eggs and coral of lobster with 1 pound butter; force through a sieve.
Wine suggestion: Medium white California wine

CHICAGO CLAIM COMPANY

ADDRESS   2314 North Clark Street
TELEPHONE   871-1770
HOURS AND DAYS   Mon. 5–11:30 P.M.;
          Tues.–Thurs. 11:30 A.M.–11:30 P.M.;
          Fri., Sat. 11:30 A.M.–12:30 A.M.;
          Sun. 3:30–10:30 P.M.
HOLIDAYS CLOSED   All major holidays
RESERVATIONS   Limited basis
CREDIT CARDS   No
ENTERTAINMENT   No
PARKING   Street
BANQUET FACILITIES   No
DRESS   Casual
LIQUOR   Yes
WINE   Limited selection

The setting of the Chicago Claim Company has an old mining atmosphere. The menus, which won the Gold Medal Menu Design Award in 1974, are printed on a prospector's mining pan. Selections are wide and include the Motherlode, a huge hamburger with a choice of many tasty toppings. A salad bar is offered, which consists of a large variety of fresh items and dressings. Several other entrees available include Chicken or Beef Teriyaki, Beef Kabob, red snapper, lobster and roast beef. The dinner price ranges from $2.65 to $9.50. The background music is rock, which attracts a young or young-at-heart crowd.

Claim Sauce

1 *gallon*

1 quart Open Pit Barbeque Sauce

3 24-ounce bottles Heinz Ketchup

2 oranges, cut up (including juice and grated rind)

2 tablespoons Worcestershire sauce

1¼ cups white vinegar

½ pound brown sugar

2 tablespoons lemon juice

Mix all ingredients and simmer for 20 minutes. Serve hot or cold over hamburgers or steaks.

CLUB EL BIANCO

ADDRESS   10067 Skokie Boulevard, Skokie
TELEPHONE   673-3131
HOURS AND DAYS   Daily noon–11 P.M.
HOLIDAYS CLOSED   July 4, Thanksgiving, Christmas
RESERVATIONS   Advisable
CREDIT CARDS   All major cards
ENTERTAINMENT   No
PARKING   Yes
BANQUET FACILITIES   Yes
DRESS   Semi-casual
LIQUOR   Yes
WINE   Good selection

Dining is a pleasure at this excellent Italian restaurant. All the food served is prepared nicely and is of a very high quality. The menu varies from the tasty spaghetti to the exceptional Chicken Vesuvio. If your group consists of hearty eaters, you should try the "Fiesta Dinner" (truly a feast). Be sure to save room for the freshly baked pastries, cookies, fruits, spumoni and nuts.

Lake Trout alla Livornese

Serves 1

3 chopped scallion tops
2 tablespoons butter
  Pinch of fresh garlic,
  chopped
  Pinch of parsley
  Pinch of oregano
  Black pepper

Juice of ¼ lemon
2 chopped anchovies
3 crushed canned tomatoes
3 ounces cooking sauterne
7- to 8-ounce piece of
  partially baked trout

Sauté scallion tops in butter along with garlic, parsley, oregano, pepper, lemon juice, anchovies and tomatoes. When the scallions are limp but not brown, drain off butter. Add the wine and the trout and cook until the wine has cooked down.

Wine suggestion: Dry white Italian wine

THE CONNOISSEUR'S
DINING ROOM

ADDRESS   7012 North Western Avenue
TELEPHONE   262-5752
HOURS AND DAYS   Daily 5:30 P.M. on
HOLIDAYS CLOSED   None
RESERVATIONS   Yes
CREDIT CARDS   Cash only
ENTERTAINMENT   No
PARKING   Yes
BANQUET FACILITIES   Will close restaurant for private parties
DRESS   Jacket and tie for men, dress for women
LIQUOR   Yes
WINE   Good selection

This small, quaint restaurant is truly unique. There is no menu. A ten-course dinner is planned for you by selecting the freshest foods available in the market that day. Each time you dine there, your name and the entrees you had are recorded for their file. This is done in order that they never duplicate your meal, unless a specific item is requested. The first dinner is standard, and after that it varies greatly. The portions are small and spaced to allow each party to dine at its own pace. The majority of dishes are prepared right at your table. The ten courses consist of an appetizer; soup; fish or seafood; salad; poultry; beef, veal or lamb; vegetable side dish; dessert; special blend coffee; and a fruit and cheese tray.

Strawberries Romanoff

Serves 4

2 tablespoons unsalted butter
1 teaspoon natural brown sugar
½ teaspoon cloves
1 teaspoon cinnamon

1 pint fresh strawberries
Juice of ½ fresh lemon
2 tablespoons Grand Marnier
2 tablespoons cognac
¼ cup sour cream
¼ cup heavy whipping cream

In a pan, place butter, brown sugar, cloves, cinnamon, strawberries, lemon juice, Grand Marnier and cognac. Heat and flame. Add sour cream and whipping cream. Mix, heat through, and serve over ice cream.

Wine suggestion: Sweet white Bordeaux or any Champagne

THE CONSORT

ADDRESS   909 North Michigan Avenue (The Continental Plaza)
TELEPHONE   943-7200, ext. 428
HOURS AND DAYS   Lunch: Mon.-Fri. noon–3:00 P.M.;
     Sun. brunch 11 A.M.–3 P.M.
     Dinner: Sun–Fri. 6 P.M.–1 A.M.; Sat. 6 P.M.–2 A.M.
HOLIDAYS CLOSED   Memorial Day, Labor Day, Christmas
RESERVATIONS   Strongly recommended
CREDIT CARDS   AE, CB, DC, MC, VI, Western International
     Hotels
ENTERTAINMENT   Franz Benteler and the Royal Strings
PARKING   In hotel
BANQUET FACILITIES   No
DRESS   Jacket and tie at dinner
LIQUOR   Yes
WINE   Extensive selection

Turn a night into a special, romantic evening by dining at the Consort. Listen to the superb music of Franz Benteler with his 1701 Stradivarius and the "Royal Strings." Dancing between courses gives even more romantic drama to the night, as does the tableside serenade. Each lady receives a red rose, a real special-occasion experience. This formal dining room is located on the 16th floor of the Continental Plaza. Its regal decor is silver, amethyst and gold. Smoke-mirrored columns are hung with ornate sconces giving light to the velvet trappings. The a la carte menu of Continental cuisine has many outstanding items to choose from. Our two favorites are the Beef Wellington and the Steak Diane. The dessert selection is outstanding. The "flamed at your table" choices include Crepes Suzette, Cherries Jubilee or the excitingly different Bananas Flambé. A magnificent dessert wagon is also available to choose from.

L'Entrecôte Orientale

Serves 4

4 10-ounce sirloin steaks
½ ounce (1 tablespoon) soy
sauce

½ ounce (1 tablespoon) fresh
shredded ginger
Sauce Orientale (see
below)

Mix the soy sauce and ginger, spread on top of steaks and set aside for 10 minutes. Then broil steaks to desired doneness and top with Sauce Orientale.

SAUCE ORIENTALE

½ ounce (1 tablespoon) soy
sauce
2 ounces (¼ cup) chicken
stock
½ ounce (1 tablespoon)
cornstarch
½ ounce (1 tablespoon)
ginger, shredded

¼ cup water chestnuts,
sliced thin
¼ cup celery, julienne sliced
¼ cup tomato (peeled with
center core removed)
2 tablespoons oil
½ ounce (1 tablespoon) sugar

Add soy sauce to chicken stock; bring to a boil. Slightly thicken with cornstarch and flavor with ginger. Sauté the water chestnuts, celery and tomato in oil in a separate pan and add to sauce. Stir in sugar.
Wine suggestion: Medium red California wine

THE COTTAGE

ADDRESS   525 Torrence Avenue, Calumet City
TELEPHONE   891-3900
HOURS AND DAYS   Tues.–Thurs. 5–10 P.M.; Fri., Sat. 5–11 P.M.
HOLIDAYS CLOSED   Varies
RESERVATIONS   Preferred
CREDIT CARDS   No
ENTERTAINMENT   No
PARKING   Yes
BANQUET FACILITIES   No
DRESS   Informal
LIQUOR   Yes
WINE   Good selection

 A jewel of a place, The Cottage is like a small country house one would find in England or France, and is furnished with antiques, a fireplace, an atrium, and objects pertaining to food and wine. The atmosphere is comfortable and homelike. Service is somewhat formal but not stuffy. Lovely fresh flowers are seen as you enter the restaurant. Jerry and Carolyn Buster add that personal loving touch in everything they do. A rarity to find these days is a woman chef. Her exceptional gourmet dinners include outstanding soups and desserts. The menu changes according to the seasons and appears on framed blackboards. Steak Viennoise (sirloin topped with twice-fried onions), Mock Lobster, rolled whitefish served with butter and Veal Florentine are recommendations to try; however, everything is great.

"The Cottage" Schnitzel

Serves 4–6

2 pounds pork tenderloin,
   trimmed of all fat and
   silverskin
Flour

Batter (see below)
Butter
Lemon juice, freshly
   squeezed

Cut tenderloin into ¼"–½" slices and pound each slice into a thin medallion approximately 3" in diameter. Dip each medallion first in flour and then in batter. Melt enough butter to cover bottom of heavy frying pan. Quickly sauté medallions in butter until browned on each side. As they are done, remove to serving tray. When all have been browned, quickly deglaze frying pan with freshly squeezed lemon juice (amount will depend on size of frying pan and amount of butter used). Pour pan juices over schnitzel and serve immediately.

BATTER

2 large eggs
2 tablespoons flour
2 tablespoons freshly grated
   Parmesan cheese
½ cup milk

Salt, white pepper,
nutmeg, and freshly
chopped parsley, according
to taste

Place all ingredients in blender container and blend together at high speed for 2 minutes.

Wine suggestion: Medium white German or California wine

COUNTRY INN OF NORTHBROOK

ADDRESS   755 Skokie Boulevard, Northbrook
TELEPHONE   498-1900
HOURS AND DAYS   Daily 11 A.M.–11 P.M.
HOLIDAYS CLOSED   None
RESERVATIONS   Preferred
CREDIT CARDS   AE, DC, MC, VI
ENTERTAINMENT   Live in the lounge, Tues.–Sat. from 7 P.M.
PARKING   Ample free parking
BANQUET FACILITIES   Small gatherings
DRESS   Optional
LIQUOR   Yes
WINE   Limited selection

A touch of England can be found in this restaurant. It is in a beautiful English setting with fireplaces, tapestry rugs, a variety of lovely and different chairs, and fresh flowers on the tables. Depending on what the market has to offer, there are nightly specials. The duckling with orange sauce and the Beef Wellington are outstanding. The fluffy chocolate mousse and the English trifle (cake soaked in wine, custard and fruit) are tasty desserts.

English Trifle with Sherry Sauce

Serves 12–15

1 9- to 10-ounce spongecake
3 tablespoons cream sherry
1¼ cups raspberry or
  strawberry preserves

1¼ quarts custard sauce (at
  room temperature)
Whipped cream topping
¼ cup julienne-sliced
  almonds, lightly toasted

Place cake in the bottom of a shallow bowl and soak with sherry. Spread preserves and custard over the cake and cover with the whipped cream topping. Sprinkle the almonds on top.

Wine suggestion: Spanish sweet sherry

COURT HOUSE

ADDRESS   5211 South Harper Street
TELEPHONE   667-4008
HOURS AND DAYS   Mon.–Thurs. 11:30 A.M.–11 P.M.; Fri. 11:30
    A.M.–midnight; Sun. 10:30 A.M.–11 P.M. Brunch: Sat.
    9:30 A.M.–noon; Sun. 9:30 A.M.–3 P.M.
HOLIDAYS CLOSED   All major holidays
RESERVATIONS   Accepted only for large parties
CREDIT CARDS   AE, MC
ENTERTAINMENT   Classical guitar (Mon., Wed. 6:30–10:30 P.M.);
    Clavichord (Tues., Thurs. 6:30–10:30 P.M.)
PARKING   Metered city lot next door
BANQUET FACILITIES   No
DRESS   Casual
LIQUOR   Yes
WINE   Good selection

This restaurant is near the University of Chicago and the Museum of Science and Industry. It was the first restaurant in the city to serve fondue. Other specialties include Beef Stroganoff and fresh whitefish. The very unique cheesecake is delicious. The lovely wood floors, tables and beamed ceiling give this restaurant a homey feeling. On Sundays, there is an excellent brunch buffet including eggs, cheese, smoked fish, cold cuts, bagels, different kinds of bread and occasionally lox. It's enough to satisfy the most hearty appetites.

Chicken Liver Pâté

1 *Party Mold*

¾ *pound fresh chicken livers*	3 *tablespoons butter*
¼ *teaspoon chopped garlic*	1½ *teaspoon brandy*
1 *tablespoon minced onion*	1½ *teaspoon dry sherry*
1 *teaspoon basil*	½ *cup melted butter*
Pinch ground cloves	½ *teaspoon anchovy paste*

Combine the first five ingredients and sauté in butter until the chicken livers are medium rare. Put into the blender with the last four ingredients and blend at a high speed until smooth. Chill in lightly buttered mold. Unmold to serve.

Wine suggestion: Dry white Bordeaux or California Sauvignon

LA CREPERIE

ADDRESS   2845 North Clark Street
TELEPHONE   528-9050
HOURS AND DAYS   Wed.–Mon. 5–11 P.M.
HOLIDAYS CLOSED   Easter, Christmas
RESERVATIONS   No
CREDIT CARDS   No
ENTERTAINMENT   Baby grand which customers may play
PARKING   At Century Parking Garage
BANQUET FACILITIES   Yes
DRESS   Casual
LIQUOR   No, but guests may bring their own
WINE   Bring your own

The chef-owner of La Creperie, a native of Brittany, uses the crepe recipes handed down in his family from generation to generation. Wheat and buckwheat crepes are prepared before your eyes. After the fresh and tasty fillings have been put on the crepe, they are folded into square shapes rather than rolled. The menu, written on a blackboard, offers many interesting selections. The spinach, cheese and mushroom crepe and the seafood crepe are our favorites. The Grand Marnier crepe is excellent and a great ending to any meal.

Chocolate Banana Crepe

Serves 1

Sweet wheat crepe
Melted butter
¼ cup chocolate chips
1 banana

2 tablespoons creme de
banana liqueur
Powdered sugar
Whipped cream

Lay the crepe flat. Place 1 tablespoon melted butter on center of crepe. Pour chocolate chips over butter. Slice banana and place over chips, reserving one slice. Pour liqueur over banana. Place 1 tablespoon melted butter on each of two diagonal corners. Put 1 tablespoon powdered sugar on each of the other corners. Fold crepe to form a square. Flip onto plate with the folds down. Add whipped cream and reserved banana slice on top and serve.

CRICKET'S

ADDRESS   100 East Chestnut Street
TELEPHONE   751-2400
HOURS AND DAYS   Lunch: Mon–Sat. 11:30 A.M.–2:30 P.M.;
          Sun. 11 A.M.–3 P.M.
          Dinner: (Daily) 5:30–10:30 P.M.
          Late supper Mon.–Sat. 10:30 P.M.–midnight
HOLIDAYS CLOSED   Christmas
RESERVATIONS   Yes
CREDIT CARDS   AE, DC, MC, VI
ENTERTAINMENT   No
PARKING   Doorman
BANQUET FACILITIES   Yes
DRESS   Jacket and tie
LIQUOR   Yes
WINE   Extensive selection

Cricket's, a newcomer to Chicago, is fast becoming the
"in" spot to dine. Their instant success is easy to understand, as
the service is friendly and the food is superb. The interior features walnut columns and beams with hanging trivia reminiscent
of an earlier Chicago. An elegant bar is adjacent to the dining
room. The style, specialties and technical know-how were provided by the famous "21" Club of New York. Some excellent
choices to consider are the seafood crepes, an outstanding spinach salad, fantastic rack of lamb or the escallopine of veal. The
rice pudding that we had for dessert was the best we've experi-
enced. A good fact to keep in mind is that Cricket's offers great
"eye openers" for Sunday brunch and late supper menus.

Burger au Cricket

Serves 3–4

2 pounds ground sirloin
¼ teaspoon nutmeg
   Dash of Worcestershire
   sauce
   Salt and freshly ground

pepper to taste
¼ cup bread crumbs
¼ cup cooked celery,
   chopped
   Oil

Preheat the oven to 350°. In a mixing bowl, combine all of the ingredients except oil by hand, using rapid motions, without overworking mixture. Shape into round patties (about 8–10 ounces each). Heat a little vegetable oil in an ovenproof skillet. When the pan is very hot, brown the patties quickly on both sides. Put the skillet in the oven and cook the meat until done to taste (about 5 minutes for rare).

Wine suggestion: Medium red Burgundy or California wine

DAI-ICHI

ADDRESS   512 South Wabash Avenue
TELEPHONE   922-5527
HOURS AND DAYS   Mon.–Fri. 11:30 A.M.–3 P.M., 5–10:30 P.M.;
            Sat. noon–11 P.M.;
            Sun. 5–9:30 P.M.
HOLIDAYS CLOSED   Christmas
RESERVATIONS   Desirable
CREDIT CARDS   AE, CB, DC
ENTERTAINMENT   No
PARKING   Lot adjacent to 512 South Wabash Avenue
BANQUET FACILITIES   From 20 to 200
DRESS   Casual
LIQUOR   Yes
WINE   Limited selection

Dai-Ichi, meaning "great number one," is the only Japanese restaurant in the United States that has won an award from the Chefs of Cuisine Association. It is authentically designed with kimono-clad geishas to serve you. The specialties are Sukiyaki, Shrimp Tempura, and Lobster Toyko style. For a special taste treat, try the Salmon Tsutsumiyaki, salmon covered in foil with spinach, tomato and onion, spiced to perfection. The interior design conveys the atmosphere of both old and new Japan, and includes a steak house setting as well as a charming garden tea house. The authentic decor, friendly service and interesting food add up to a very enjoyable dining experience.

Authentic Sukiyaki

Serves 4

1 pound tender cut of beef
1 pound hakusai (Japanese
   cabbage), sliced diagonally
4 green onions, sliced
   diagonally
8 medium mushrooms,
   sliced

8 soy bean cakes, each 1" x
   2"
   Soy sauce
8 teaspoons sugar
8 tablespoons saki (Japanese
   wine)
4 eggs

Slice beef thinly into an iron pot. Add all the vegetables, then add 2½ cups soy sauce, sugar and saki. Place pot over high heat and boil for 5 minutes. Serve in same pot, with 4 side dishes of 1 raw egg each. Provide soy sauce for adding to egg as it is scrambled. This is used as a dipping sauce for the Sukiyaki. A bowl of white rice makes a nice complement to this dish.

Wine suggestion: Japanese saki or beer, or a medium white German wine

DEL RIO

ADDRESS   228 Greenbay Road, Highwood
TELEPHONE   432-4608
HOURS AND DAYS   Mon.–Sat. 5–11 P.M.
HOLIDAYS CLOSED   All major holidays
RESERVATIONS   No
CREDIT CARDS   No
ENTERTAINMENT   No
PARKING   In rear
BANQUET FACILITIES   No
DRESS   Casual
LIQUOR   Yes
WINE   Extensive selection

This outstanding Italian restaurant in Highwood is family owned and operated. In this friendly, bustling atmosphere be prepared for a short wait. However, cocktails are served, and there is complimentary hot garlic bread available to help pass the time. The food is worth the wait, especially the delicious strip steaks, veal and eggplant Parmesan, and the Ravioli Alforno. This is a place to which you will love to return, a longtime North Shore favorite.

Frittata Del Rio

Serves 6

12 *large, fresh eggs, beaten*
¼ *cup heavy cream*
¼ *pound butter, melted*
  Salt, pepper and nutmeg
  to taste

½ *cup grated Parmesan*
  cheese
  Filling (see below)
1 *cup diced mozzarella*
  cheese

Scramble the eggs with the cream, melted butter, seasonings and ¼ cup of the Parmesan cheese. Put eggs in an ovenproof casserole and pour the filling over them. Sprinkle with the rest of the Parmesan cheese and put the mozzarella cheese on top. Put under broiler or in a 500° oven for 10 minutes.

FILLING

1 *cup mushrooms, cut in*
  pieces
1 *cup green pepper, diced*
½ *bermuda onion, diced*
8 *small peeled tomatoes,*
  cut into quarters (use
  canned if fresh not

  available)
2 *cloves garlic*
  Salt and pepper
1 *tablespoon rosemary,*
  ground
¼ *cup olive oil*
¼ *cup butter*

Cook all the vegetables and seasonings in the oil and butter for 25 minutes.
Wine suggestion: Dry white Italian wine

DIANNA'S RESTAURANT OPAA

ADDRESS   212 South Halsted Street
TELEPHONE   332-1225
HOURS AND DAYS   Daily 11 A.M.–2 A.M.
HOLIDAYS CLOSED   None
RESERVATIONS   Not necessary
CREDIT CARDS   AE
ENTERTAINMENT   Greek dancing by Petros
PARKING   Free, across the street
BANQUET FACILITIES   Yes
DRESS   Casual
LIQUOR   Yes
WINE   Limited selection

      Dianna's Opaa is decorated in a village-type setting and is located in the midst of exciting Greek Town. The atmosphere is comfortable and happy as there is usually a happy occasion being celebrated. While dining on tasty authentic cuisine, you will be entertained by the great Greek dancing of Petros, the owner. The menu lists all items in Greek and English. The flaming cheese delicacy, spinach cheese pie, and dolmades (stuffed grape leaves) are all truly delicious.

Saganaki (Flaming Cheese)

Serves 1

1 *piece of kasseri or
kefalotyri cheese, cut in a
triangle*
1 *egg*
Flour

Oil or butter
1 *whiskey glass of Metaxa or
other brandy*
½ *lemon*

Dip cheese into beaten egg, flour it and then fry it in an oiled or buttered frying pan, turning it over twice. Have a hot pan ready and put the cheese in it. Pour the brandy on the cheese and light it with a match. Extinguish the flames by squeezing the lemon over the pan.

Wine suggestion: Greek rosé

DINGBAT'S

ADDRESS   247 East Ontario Street
TELEPHONE   751-1337
HOURS AND DAYS   Lunch: Daily from 11 A.M.
        Dinner: Sun.–Thurs. 4 P.M.–midnight;
        Fri., Sat. 4 P.M.–2 A.M.
HOLIDAYS CLOSED   July 4, Labor Day, Thanksgiving
RESERVATIONS   Recommended on weekends
CREDIT CARDS   All major cards
ENTERTAINMENT   Piano bar 4-10 P.M.; Disco dancing
PARKING   Valet parking after 6 P.M.
BANQUET FACILITIES   Yes
DRESS   Casual
LIQUOR   Yes
WINE   Limited selection

This exciting, fun spot for dining and disco dancing is located on the site of the former Chez Paree. The slick white sculptured interior is highlighted with graphics, neon art and colorful abstract paintings. The music is fabulous, whether it be the background selections, the delightful voice at the piano bar or the wild disco sounds. A stainless steel disco room gives diners a good view of the action. The menu is full of unique specialties at very reasonable prices. A second menu is always available for those who wish a lighter meal. Everything that we ordered was truly delicious. Batter Up, a variety of french-fried vegetables, proved to be an interesting and tasty appetizer. The gazpacho soup, crab legs and ribs were all thoroughly enjoyed.

Steak Florentine

Serves 5

4 tablespoons chopped parsley	1 clove garlic, chopped
1 teaspoon oregano	½ teaspoon black pepper
1 teaspoon basil	5 12-ounce strip steaks
½ teaspoon thyme	10 mushroom caps
4 tablespoons olive oil	1 teaspoon butter
1½ teaspoons MSG (monosodium glutamate)	1 cup red wine

Mix the herbs, oil, MSG, garlic and pepper to make a marinade. Wrap steaks in foil with marinade and refrigerate for 24 hours. Broil steaks, still wrapped in foil, to desired doneness. In small frying pan, sauté the mushrooms in butter. Splash with red wine and juices from the steaks. Serve mushroom caps with steak.

Wine suggestion: Medium red California wine

DON'S FISHMARKET AND
PROVISION COMPANY

ADDRESS   9335 Skokie Boulevard, Skokie
TELEPHONE   677-3424
HOURS AND DAYS   Lunch: Mon.–Fri. 11:30 A.M.–2:30 P.M.
          Dinner: Mon.–Thurs. 5–11 P.M.; Fri., Sat. 5 P.M.–
          midnight; Sun. 4–10:30 P.M.
HOLIDAYS CLOSED   Dinner only on all holidays. Closed
          Christmas and New Year's Day.
RESERVATIONS   Advisable
CREDIT CARDS   AE, MC, VI
ENTERTAINMENT   No
PARKING   Yes
BANQUET FACILITIES   No
DRESS   Casual
LIQUOR   Yes
WINE   Limited house wines

This is a popular and crowded restaurant. Make your
reservations well in advance. A generous salad with chunky blue
cheese dressing or tiny bay shrimp is served on pewter plates.
The crock of New England clam chowder is a must for fish
lovers. Several "specials" every day usually include a salt-water
fish and a shellfish selection. The broad menu has all your favorites, from Boston scrod to live lobster. Watch them cook it
through a large glass window in the kitchen. A "Don's bucket for
two," containing two lobsters, crab, mussels, corn and redskins,
is delicious and extremely filling. The greatest hot bialy bread,
served with whipped butter, is included with your meal. The
setting is rustic with very friendly service.

Crabmeat and Grape Stuffing

Serves 4

½ cup mushrooms, sliced
⅓ cup onion, chopped
⅓ cup celery, diced
10 ounces (1¼ cups) King
   crabmeat
4 ounces (1 stick) butter
½ teaspoon salt

1 teaspoon black pepper
4 ounces (½ cup) white
   wine
1 tablespoon thyme
1 bay leaf
1 cup medium white sauce
½ cup grapes

Sauté vegetables with crabmeat in butter. Add salt and pepper, wine, thyme and bay leaf. Boil. Add white sauce and grapes. Use to stuff trout.

Wine suggestion: Medium white German wine

DORO'S

ADDRESS   871 North Rush Street
TELEPHONE   266-1414
HOURS AND DAYS   Lunch: Mon.–Fri. 11:30 A.M.–2:30 P.M.
         Dinner: Mon.–Sat. 6–11 P.M.
HOLIDAYS CLOSED   All major holidays
RESERVATIONS   Yes
CREDIT CARDS   AE, CB, DC, VI
ENTERTAINMENT   Piano
PARKING   Doorman
BANQUET FACILITIES   No
DRESS   Jacket
LIQUOR   Yes
WINE   Extensive selection

This is an exceedingly pleasant restaurant serving exciting and fabulous northern Italian food. The high quality pastas are made by a special machine, reportedly one of only three in the Chicago area. Wait till you taste the marvelous fettucine, cannelloni, lasagna and ravioli. The veal is of the finest caliber and is cooked to perfection. You can't go wrong ordering anything here. Our suggestions for dinner include Minestrone Soup (tasty vegetables), Suprema Di Pollo Bolognese (chicken with prosciutto and cheese), Risotto Ai Piselli and Scampi (rice with peas and shrimp), Pesce Del Lago Alla Griglia (whitefish) and Piccata Lombarda (veal with white wine, lemon and butter). A happy ending to a delicious meal is their zabaglione (egg yolks, sugar and marsala), cooked at your table.

Costoletta Valtostana (Stuffed Veal Chops)

Serves 2

2 veal rib chops (frenched
and butterflied, perhaps by
butcher)
2 slices of muenster or
mozzarella cheese
2 thin slices of prosciutto
2 tablespoons grated
Parmesan cheese
Flour
1 egg, well beaten

2 tablespoons oil
5 tablespoons butter
1–2 ounces white wine
1 teaspoon chopped parsley
2 ounces (¼ cup) chicken
stock
2 ounces (¼ cup) brown
gravy (may substitute
beef stock)
Double pinch of salt

Preheat oven to 400°. Open veal chops on work table, cover
with wax paper and pound them with flat object. Remove paper.
Lay a slice of cheese, a slice of prosciutto, and a sprinkle of
grated cheese on one half of each chop, then fold other half of
chop over and pat down. Flour both chops and dip in egg. Combine oil and 2 tablespoons butter in ovenproof pan over
medium-high heat. When heated, slip chops into pan. Cook
until chops are brown (about 2 minutes) and turn over. Cook an
additional minute, then place in oven for approximately 20 minutes. Remove pan from oven and pour off liquid. Place pan back
on medium burner. Add wine, parsley, remaining 3 tablespoons
butter, chicken stock, brown gravy and salt. Let simmer for a
few minutes to enhance flavor.

Wine suggestion: Medium red Italian wine

DRAGON INN NORTH

ADDRESS   1650 Waukegan Road, Glenview
TELEPHONE   729-8383
HOURS AND DAYS   Tues.–Thurs. 11:30 A.M.–10 P.M.; Fri. 11:30
       A.M.–midnight; Sat. 5 P.M.–midnight
HOLIDAYS CLOSED   Thanksgiving, Christmas, New Year's Day
RESERVATIONS   Weekends
CREDIT CARDS   AE
ENTERTAINMENT   No
PARKING   Free private lot
BANQUET FACILITIES   Small groups (20–30) except Saturday
DRESS   Casual
LIQUOR   Yes
WINE   Limited selection
OTHER LOCATIONS   Dragon Inn, 18431 S. Halsted, Glenwood,
       756-3344
       Dragon Seed, 2300 N. Lincoln Park West, 528-5542

Aside from the fabulous food, the most unique aspect of this restaurant is Susan Sih, the owner. She is a vibrant, charming woman with many interesting stories to share. Specialties of the house are spring rolls, steamed dumplings, Szechuan Diced Chicken, crispy duck, Moo Shoo Pork (delectable shredded pork, egg, vegetables and plum sauce rolled into a crepe), Hot and Sour Soup and the sizzling Golden Rice Soup. This restaurant is a WBBM Dining Award winner for the years 1974–1975. Go with a group—it's fun.

Szechuan Diced Chicken

Serves 2

1 pound boned chicken,
  diced into ¼" cubes
1 egg white, unbeaten
1 teaspoon cornstarch
6 tablespoons vegetable oil
½ cup hot, dried peppers

1 tablespoon cooking sherry
1 teaspoon sugar
3 tablespoons soy sauce
1 cup dry-roasted peanuts
1 green onion, chopped

Mix diced chicken with egg white and cornstarch. Heat oil in wok (or frying pan) over high heat—but watch carefully to prevent scorching. Sauté dried peppers for 30 seconds. Dump in diced chicken and stir-fry until chicken turns white. Add sherry, sugar and soy sauce, stirring continuously, then add peanuts. Mix well and quickly in wok. Garnish with green onion and serve hot with steamed rice.

Wine suggestion: Medium white or medium red California wine

E'LA CUM INN

ADDRESS   514 Main Street, Evanston
TELEPHONE   864-3533
HOURS AND DAYS   Mon.–Thurs. 11 A.M.–11 P.M.; Fri. 11 A.M.–
         midnight; Sat. 4 P.M.–midnight; Sun. 4–10 P.M.
HOLIDAYS CLOSED   Memorial Day, July 4, Labor Day,
         Christmas
RESERVATIONS   Yes
CREDIT CARDS   AE, DC, MC,
ENTERTAINMENT   Occasionally
PARKING   In bank parking lot after bank hours (Bank of
               Evanston)
BANQUET FACILITIES   No
DRESS   Casual
LIQUOR   Yes
WINE   Limited selection

This is a good Greek restaurant where it is possible to get a nice variety of authentic Greek dishes. It is attractively decorated with large private booths. Lively recorded Greek music creates a spirited atmosphere. The spinach and cheese pie with its flaky crust is fantastic. The moussaka is delicious, moist, and nicely seasoned. Although the salad bar is small, everything on it is fresh and tasty. The service is very helpful and warm.

Moussaka

Serves 10–12

1 *pound plus 4 tablespoons
   (4½ sticks) butter*
4 *cups flour*
½ *gallon milk, heated*

1 *cup plus 6 tablespoons of
   kefalotyri or Parmesan
   cheese, grated*
Salt, pepper and nutmeg

98

3 *medium eggplants*	3 *pounds ground beef*
3 *medium potatoes*	3 *tablespoons brandy*
3 *medium green squash*	1 *cup tomato paste*
Oil	¾ *cup dry bread crumbs*
1 *large onion, chopped fine*	2 *eggs*

To make the white sauce (béchamel), melt 1 pound butter in a saucepan. Add flour gradually, and stirring constantly. Then add milk, slowly, simmering for 5 minutes or until it resembles a cottage cheese consistency. Remove from heat and add ½ cup cheese, and salt, pepper and nutmeg to taste; stir very well.

Slice eggplants, potatoes and squash, rinse and sprinkle with a little salt. Fry them in oil to a golden brown. Generously grease a 13 x 9-inch pan and sprinkle it with grated cheese. Place vegetables in three layers inside pan, starting with the eggplant, then the potatoes and last, the green squash. Meanwhile, fry the onion in 1 tablespoon butter, to a golden brown; add beef and cook for 15–20 minutes. Add brandy and tomato paste, season to taste with pepper, salt and nutmeg, cover pan and simmer for an additional 15–20 minutes. Remove from heat and let stand for 5 minutes. If grease forms on top, remove with a spoon. Add bread crumbs, ½ cup cheese and eggs. Mix well and place the mixture on top of layered vegetables. Sprinkle top with 3 tablespoons of cheese, cover with the white sauce evenly and sprinkle with an additional 3 tablespoons of cheese. Melt remaining 3 tablespoons butter and spread over all with a brush. Bake for 15–20 minutes at 375°–400°, until a golden brown. Cool slightly and cut into squares. Note: Seasonings can be altered to taste.

Wine suggestion: Very dry white Bordeaux or California wine

ELI'S, THE PLACE FOR STEAK

ADDRESS   215 East Chicago Avenue
TELEPHONE   642-1393
HOURS AND DAYS   Lunch: Mon.–Fri. 11 A.M.–2:30 P.M.
          Dinner: Daily 4 P.M.–midnight
HOLIDAYS CLOSED   All major holidays
RESERVATIONS   Yes
CREDIT CARDS   AE
ENTERTAINMENT   Piano bar
PARKING   Garage inside building
BANQUET FACILITIES   No
DRESS   Jacket
LIQUOR   Yes
WINE   Good selection

"We shall serve good food here—at a profit, if we can, at a loss, if we must, but always good food." Those are the words on Eli's menu, which explains why the restaurant has remained a popular favorite for over ten years. Specializing in steaks and prime ribs, Eli's is also known for its superb calf's liver and Shrimp Marc, named after Eli's son. The Italian Pepper Steak is large slices of beef tenderloin with mushrooms, tomatoes and green peppers in a fantastic wine sauce. After you've tried this dish, you'll have a difficult time finding a comparable one anywhere. It's definitely a favorite. All entrees include salad and a baked potato or an order of Eli's fabulous cottage fries. The brandy ice makes a delightful and refreshing dessert. Try their intimate piano bar for a cocktail before or after dinner.

Eli's Chopped Liver

3 cups

1 *pound chicken livers*	2 *hard-cooked eggs*
2 *medium onions, chopped*	1 *teaspoon salt*
⅓ *cup rendered chicken fat*	½ *teaspoon pepper*

Boil livers in water to cover until no pink remains. Sauté onion in chicken fat until golden brown. Chop livers, onion and eggs coarsely and evenly, or put through food grinder. (Do not use electric blender.) Gently stir in salt and pepper; refrigerate. Serve garnished with chopped egg and parsley sprigs. Also good spread on thin crackers or toast.

Wine suggestion: Spanish, California or New York State dry sherry

EPICUREAN

ADDRESS   316 South Wabash Avenue
TELEPHONE   WE9-2190
HOURS AND DAYS   Mon.–Sat. 11 A.M.–9 P.M.
HOLIDAYS CLOSED   All national holidays
RESERVATIONS   Not necessary
CREDIT CARDS   AE, MC, VI
ENTERTAINMENT   No
PARKING   Free with dinner, two doors south of restaurant
BANQUET FACILITIES   Yes
DRESS   Casual
LIQUOR   Yes
WINE   Small selection

Epicurean, specializing in Hungarian and Continental cuisine, has been in existence for 38 years. It's not a fancy place, but it's impressive for its warm atmosphere. The food is also impressive. Their outstanding Hungarian specialties include excellent Hungarian Beef Goulash and smoked Hungarian sausage served with sauerkraut. For a taste sampling of several dishes, try their famous Taster Platter consisting of Chicken Paprikash, Beef Goulash and Szekely Goulash. The menu also offers a good selection of chicken, seafood and beef.

Hungarian Beef Goulash

Serves 6–8

1½ pounds onions, diced
¼ cup shortening
2 tablespoons Hungarian paprika
2 tablespoons anise seeds
1 teaspoon coarsely ground garlic

3 pounds boneless chuck or round steak
1 pint beef broth
Salt and black pepper to taste
Flour

Sauté onions in shortening until transparent; add paprika, anise seeds, and garlic. Then add the meat, beef broth, salt and pepper. Bring to a simmer and cover. Cook until meat is tender, then thicken with a flour and water paste until you have a smooth gravy. Serve with buttered noodles, rice or potatoes.

Wine suggestion: Medium red Hungarian wine

EUGENE'S

ADDRESS   1255 North State Street
TELEPHONE   944-1445
HOURS AND DAYS   Mon.–Thurs. 5 P.M.–2 A.M.; Fri., Sat.
    5 P.M.–3 A.M.; Sun. 5–11 P.M.
HOLIDAYS CLOSED   All national holidays
RESERVATIONS   Accepted
CREDIT CARDS   All major cards
ENTERTAINMENT   Yes
PARKING   Doorman
BANQUET FACILITIES   Luncheon only
DRESS   Jacket until 11 P.M.
LIQUOR   Yes
WINE   Good selection

Eugene's is an attractive, fun place. There's a lively bar area with great entertainment until closing. The extensive and amusing menu ranges from the Big Max—a foot-long hot dog with chili—to the Chateaubriand. There is an excellent variety of soups, salads, beef and fish, all unusually titled. Their french-fried onion rings or zucchini are a pleasing accompaniment with any meal.

Beef Back Ribs

Serves 6

1 cup chopped onions
1 cup chopped carrots
2 tablespoons salt
Pepper to taste
1 thyme leaf
½ teaspoon rosemary

1 bay leaf
Beef bones for stock
6 pounds beef back ribs
Barbecue sauce (your own
or commercial) or oil, salt
and pepper

Make the stock pot with onions, carrots, salt, pepper, thyme leaf, rosemary and bay leaf. Add the beef bones and enough water to cover, and cook on top of stove for a minimum of 2 hours (4 is better). Then add the beef back ribs. When the meat is tender, remove the ribs and lay them on a sheet pan. Brush the ribs with barbecue sauce or, if they are to be served au jus, brush with oil to which salt and pepper have been added. Bake in a 400° oven for ten minutes, turning, or broil or grill them on each side.

Wine suggestion: Medium red Rhône, Burgundy or California wine

FARMER'S DAUGHTER

ADDRESS   14455 La Grange Road, Orland Park
TELEPHONE   349-2330
HOURS AND DAYS   Mon.–Sat. 5–11 P.M.; Sun. 2–8 P.M.
HOLIDAYS CLOSED   Christmas Eve and Christmas
RESERVATIONS   Yes
CREDIT CARDS   AE, CB, DC, MC, VI
ENTERTAINMENT   No
PARKING   Yes, free
BANQUET FACILITIES   Up to 50; no weekends
DRESS   Jacket
LIQUOR   Yes
WINE   Limited selection

Step into this setting and enjoy two charming rooms—
the main dining room in brick and copper decor, and the Me-
són Madrid dining room in old Spanish decor with pewter settings. This restaurant is the winner of 35 international awards,
including the *Holiday* Award 1971–1977. Their specialties include Filet Au Poivre, Poached Dover Sole, London Broil,
Prime Ribs, Tornedos Dijon and all their own (some 25) homemade desserts. Everything here is well prepared and delicious.
Especially outstanding are the different soups offered every day.
The soup is left on the table in a large copper tureen, as is the
salad bowl, which offers you the opportunity to be creative with
lettuce, raw vegetables, homemade dressings and croutons. This
restaurant can be summed up in three words: "elegant country
dining."

Irish Whiskey Pie

Serves 6–8

1½ teaspoons unflavored
    gelatin
½ cup cold water
2 squares (1 ounce each)
    unsweetened chocolate
½ cup hot water
¼ teaspoon salt
½ cup sugar

¼ cup egg yolks (about 3)
¼ cup milk
3 tablespoons Irish whiskey
¼ cup egg whites (about 3)
1 cup heavy cream, whipped
¼ cup sliced almonds
1 9" chilled baked pastry
    shell

Dissolve the gelatin in cold water and put aside. Combine chocolate with hot water, salt and sugar. Bring to a boil and cook until smooth. Mix egg yolks and milk and stir into chocolate mixture. Melt gelatin over hot water until clear and add to chocolate mixture with the whiskey. Pour into mixing bowl and place over crushed ice until it becomes thick, like syrup. Beat egg whites until stiff and fold into mixture. Fold in whipped cream and almonds. Pour into pie shell and chill for 4 hours. Garnish with additional whipped cream and almonds.

Drink suggestion: Irish coffee

FEBO RESTAURANT

ADDRESS   2501 South Western Avenue
TELEPHONE   523-0839
HOURS AND DAYS   Mon.–Thurs. 11 A.M.–11 P.M.; Fri., Sat.
       11 A.M.–midnight
HOLIDAYS CLOSED   All major holidays
RESERVATIONS   Yes
CREDIT CARDS   House card only
ENTERTAINMENT   No
PARKING   Yes
BANQUET FACILITIES   From 10 to 50
DRESS   Casual
LIQUOR   Yes
WINE   Good selection

Febo means goddess of the sun, which is the symbol of warmth, in Roman mythology. The restaurant seems to generate the same feeling. The authentic Italian cooking, which takes place in their old-world atmosphere, is great and reasonably priced. Your dinner entree includes an appetizer, soup, potato, salad and dessert. The Linguine Alfredo was a delicious choice. Also enjoyed were the Chicken Vesuvio and the strip sirloin. If you have a party of four or more, call ahead for the Fiesta Dinner or, for a more sophisticated meal, request the Northern Italian dinner. They are equally delicious and the food is plentiful.

Breaded Veal Cutlet Parmesan

Serves 2

1 pound top quality veal
cutlets, center cut from
leg
¾ cup flour
3 eggs, slightly beaten
¾ cup bread crumbs
Cooking oil

1 8-ounce can tomato sauce
1 3- or 4-ounce can
mushroom pieces and
stems
Parmesan cheese
Paprika
Butter

Slice veal thinly, then pound each slice until thin and flat. Dip veal slices in flour. Dip floured veal in eggs and then in bread crumbs. Heat oil in skillet to a depth of 1″. Add cutlets; they should float in skillet. Cook and turn until both sides are golden brown. Preheat oven to 300°. Pour tomato sauce into a glass oven dish. Place cutlets on top. Put 1 tablespoon mushrooms and 2 teaspoons Parmesan cheese on each cutlet. Sprinkle with paprika; add one small slice of butter on top of each cutlet. Bake for 20 minutes.

Wine suggestion: California Sauvignon Blanc or French Pouilly-Fumé

LE FESTIVAL

ADDRESS   28 West Elm Street
TELEPHONE   944-7090
HOURS AND DAYS   Mon.–Fri. 5:30–10:30 P.M.; Sat. 5:30–11 P.M.
HOLIDAYS CLOSED   Christmas Eve, New Year's Day
RESERVATIONS   Suggested
CREDIT CARDS   AE, MC, VI
ENTERTAINMENT   Pianist
PARKING   Doorman
BANQUET FACILITIES   Up to 100
DRESS   Jacket
LIQUOR   Yes
WINE   Extensive selection

Fine china, fresh flowers, paintings and Oriental rugs lend an air of elegance to the European atmosphere of Le Festival, located in a one-hundred-year-old mansion. The superb French cuisine you will experience is prepared by the world-renowned chef Kenji Nonaka. Some of the items that we've enjoyed are the seafood coquille, Quiche Lorraine, duck in orange sauce, veal Florentine, rack of lamb and the poached turbot with hollandaise sauce. The intimacy of the first-floor bar makes it an excellent place for a drink before or after dinner.

Carbonnades Flamande

Serves 6

3 pounds beef shoulder
  Salt and pepper
  Vegetable oil
5 medium onions, thinly
  sliced
2 12-ounce bottles beer

Bouquet garni (fresh
parsley, thyme and bay
leaves tied together)
2 quarts veal stock (see
  below)
  Cornstarch

Cut meat into 12 thin slices across the grain. Season to taste with salt and pepper. Brown meat in ovenproof pan in oil over high heat. Remove meat from pan. Brown onions in same pan. Add meat, beer, bouquet garni and veal stock to pan. Cover and bake in 350° oven for 1½ hours. Thicken sauce with cornstarch diluted in very little water. Serve with buttered noodles or boiled potatoes.

VEAL STOCK

To make 2 quarts, combine 2 pounds veal bones, 1 carrot, 1 onion, 1 celery stalk (all chopped), a sprig of fresh thyme, 2–3 bay leaves, 3 ounces tomato paste and 2 gallons water in pot. Bring to a boil and simmer slowly for 3 hours, uncovered. Liquid should reduce to 2 quarts. Strain before using.

Wine suggestion: Medium red Rhône, California, New York State or Hungarian wine

FOND DE LA TOUR

ADDRESS   40 North Tower Road, Oak Brook
TELEPHONE   620-1500
HOURS AND DAYS   Lunch: Tues.–Fri. 11:30 A.M.–2 P.M.
        Dinner: Tues.–Sat. 6–11 P.M.; Sun. 4–10 P.M.
HOLIDAYS CLOSED   Memorial Day, July 4, Labor Day,
        Christmas Eve, New Year's Day
RESERVATIONS   Yes
CREDIT CARDS   All major cards
ENTERTAINMENT   No
PARKING   Valet parking available
BANQUET FACILITIES   No
DRESS   Jacket or leisure suit
LIQUOR   Yes
WINE   Good selection

This romantic, intimate restaurant with unusual decor is enhanced by an enlarged graphic representation of Seurat's "Sunday in the Park." It is small, with only 72 seats, which are clustered around a French kiosk. Favorite selections from the menu include appetizers such as Coquilles St. Jacques (made in an interesting way with fresh spinach and Sauce Perigourdine) and a dish of petite crayfish in fish sauce. The outstanding entrees are the turbot and sweetbreads. For fine dining and a relaxing evening, you'll enjoy this spot.

Gratin d'Écrevisses Glacé (Crayfish)

Serves 1

2–3 cups fish stock
  1 cup heavy cream
  8 Danish crayfish tails
    Salt and pepper
  3 tablespoons clarified
    butter

1 jigger cognac or
  almondine brandy
2 tablespoons Hollandaise
  Sauce (see below)
1 tablespoon whipped cream

Simmer the fish stock and cream for 15–20 minutes. Add crayfish tails and simmer for 5 additional minutes. Add salt and pepper to taste. Remove the crayfish, cool slightly, slit shells on the under section of tail and remove the meat. Heat butter in a saucepan and, when very hot, add the meat of the fish. Sauté until cooked and heated through. Add the cognac or brandy. Stir in the Hollandaise Sauce and whipped cream. Mix together and pour into an au gratin dish. Place under broiler until light brown (about 3 minutes). Garnish with parsley.

HOLLANDAISE SAUCE

2 egg yolks
1 tablespoon cream
½ tablespoon lemon juice

Pinch of salt
Pinch of cayenne pepper
¼ pound butter

Place egg yolks, cream, lemon juice, salt and cayenne pepper in bowl. Set bowl in a pan of hot water. Beat over a low heat until thickens. Gradually add butter, beating constantly, until it is all beaten in.

Wine suggestion: Medium white California wine

LA FONTAINE

ADDRESS   2442 North Clark Street
TELEPHONE   525-1800
HOURS AND DAYS   Lunch: Tues.–Fri. 11:30 A.M.–2:30 P.M.
            Dinner: Mon.–Sat. 5:30–10:30 P.M.
HOLIDAYS CLOSED   All major holidays
RESERVATIONS   Yes
CREDIT CARDS   AE, DC, MC, VI
ENTERTAINMENT   No
PARKING   Across the street in garage
BANQUET FACILITIES   Small parties
DRESS   Jacket
LIQUOR   Yes
WINE   Extensive selection

Excellent service, superb food and a romantic setting are all found inside this tastefully redecorated brownstone. There are many delicious specialties to try while listening to the authentic French background music which plays constantly. Strongly recommended for a great dinner are La Delice de La Fontaine (crouton, fresh mushrooms and ham covered with a mornay sauce), the thick, cheesy onion soup, the veal sautéed with applejack or the sirloin sautéed with shallots. These dishes are consistently fantastic. Occasionally we deviate from these dishes and have been pleasantly satisfied with our choices. The Quiche Lorraine, Seafood Coquille or pea soup are perfect choices for a first course. The roast duck, served with peaches and orange sauce, and the rack of lamb are excellent. Finish your meal with one of their tempting French desserts. The price of this unforgettable meal is set at $12.50 per person, with additional charges for specific items.

Veal Sauté Normande

Serves 6

1 pound veal tenderloin	½ cup dry white wine
Salt	1 pint whipping cream
Black pepper	White pepper
Oil	1 pound fresh mushrooms,
1 tablespoon butter	sliced (reserve 3 for
½ cup chopped shallots	garnish)
3 tablespoons applejack	⅓ cup chopped fresh parsley

Cut veal into 12 thin pieces; season with salt and black pepper to taste. Cover bottom of large skillet with oil and get it very hot. Add veal slices and brown on each side. Remove veal to serving dish and keep warm. Add butter to pan and melt. Add shallots and cook while stirring in the brown bits clinging to the pan. Add applejack and flame. Add white wine and reduce it until the pan is nearly dry. Add cream and simmer until it reduces and thickens. Add salt and white pepper to taste. Sauté mushrooms in oil, but do not brown. Strain the sauce into the mushrooms. Pour the sauce over the veal and garnish with cooked, whole mushrooms and parsley. Serve at once.

Wine suggestion: Dry white Burgundy

FOUR TORCHES

ADDRESS   1960 North Lincoln Park West
TELEPHONE   248-5505
HOURS AND DAYS   Lunch: Mon.–Fri. 11 A.M.–4 P.M.
    Sun. brunch 11 A.M.–4 P.M.
    Dinner: Mon.–Thurs. 5 P.M.–1 A.M.;
    Fri. till 2 A.M.; Sat. till 3 A.M.;
    Sun. till midnight
HOLIDAYS CLOSED   Christmas Eve, Christmas, New Year's Day
RESERVATIONS   Yes
CREDIT CARDS   AE, CB, MC, VI
ENTERTAINMENT   Nightly (no cover, no minimum)
PARKING   Attendant
BANQUET FACILITIES   Yes
DRESS   Jacket required for dinner only
LIQUOR   Yes
WINE   Extensive selection

The Four Torches is beautifully decorated in earth colors, fresh plants and contemporary furnishings. They have won awards from the Restaurant Association, *Hospitality* magazine and other organizations. It's usually a sure spot to find top celebrities, such as Frank Sinatra or Tom Jones, after their theater hours. For a perfect and satisfying dinner have the Grecian Salad, served with lots of feta cheese, and the peppercorn steak. Finish it off with the brandied ice topped with strawberries for a real treat.

Beef Colbert

Serves 1

8 ounces tenderloin (filet
mignon)
Salt and pepper
MSG (monosodium
glutamate)
Oil
½ clove garlic, diced
Oregano
½ cup Burgundy

½ teaspoon Worcestershire
sauce
2 teaspoons Escoffier Sauce
Diable
Brown sauce: prepared
brown gravy mix flavored
with Maggi seasoning
Wild rice

Slice tenderloin in half and season with salt, pepper and MSG.
Heat oil in sauté pan and cook meat to liking. Pour off oil and
add garlic and oregano. Pour in Burgundy. Add the Worcestershire sauce, Escoffier Sauce Diable and 2 ounces (¼ cup) of the
brown sauce. Simmer for 3 minutes. Serve with wild rice.
*Wine suggestion: Dry red Bordeaux, Burgundy or California
wine, or any of the medium "Mountain" reds*

LE FRANCAIS

ADDRESS   269 South Milwaukee Avenue, Wheeling
TELEPHONE   541-7470
HOURS AND DAYS   Tues.–Sun. 6–10 P.M.
HOLIDAYS CLOSED   Christmas
RESERVATIONS   Yes
CREDIT CARDS   AE, MC, VI
ENTERTAINMENT   No
PARKING   Valet—attendant
BANQUET FACILITIES   No
DRESS   Jacket
LIQUOR   Yes
WINE   Extensive selection

Jean and Doris Banchet, a lovely, talented couple, run this glorious restaurant. He is a Frenchman and she is German. They serve classic French cuisine. Jean is an artist in the kitchen. He loves his work, and it comes through in his delicious cooking and food presentations. They have their own bakery on the premises. The emphasis is on preparing food to a degree of perfection that bears the toughest scrutiny. Your memorable feast might include fresh bay scallops, Dover sole with lobster mousse and their special salad; don't forget to ask about their fresh baked desserts of the day. There is a comprehensive wine list. A real experience in fine dining. If you have leftovers, they are even put into aluminium foil, twisted and shaped into various object forms and ready for you to take home. You'll also take home the memories of picture-perfect trays and carts of true gourmet foods. These foods range from pâtés to desserts and are presented by your waiter for your selection.

Bisque de Homard Robert (Lobster Bisque with Saffron)

Serves 12 or more

2 *large lobsters*
  Clarified butter
1 *4-ounce glass cognac*
1 *medium onion*
2 *carrots*
6 *shallots*
1 *leek*
1 *stalk celery*
¼ *teaspoon thyme, 2 bay leaves*
  Pinch of cayenne

6 *fresh tomatoes*
4 *tablespoons tomato paste*
  Pinch of tarragon
  Pinch of saffron
2 *quarts fish stock*
1 *pint dry white wine*
  Roux made from ½ cup flour and 6 tablespoons butter
1 *quart heavy cream*

Cut the lobsters in small pieces, sauté in clarified butter and flame with ½ the glass of cognac. Remove from heat, reserve a few bits of meat for garnish, and add finely chopped onion, carrots, shallots, leek, celery, thyme, bay leaves, cayenne, tomatoes and tomato paste. Cook all ingredients for a few minutes, then add tarragon and saffron. Add fish stock and white wine. Cook for 20 minutes. Add a little roux to thicken slightly. Strain everything and add the fresh heavy cream. Add the rest of the cognac and garnish with the reserved lobster. Serve very hot.

Wine suggestion: Portuguese Vinho Verde

FRITZ, THAT'S IT!

ADDRESS   1615 Chicago Avenue, Evanston
TELEPHONE   866-8506
HOURS AND DAYS   Mon.–Thurs. 11:30 A.M.–midnight; Fri., Sat.
   11:30 A.M.–1 A.M.; Sun. 10 A.M.–midnight
HOLIDAYS CLOSED   Thanksgiving, Christmas
RESERVATIONS   No
CREDIT CARDS   No
ENTERTAINMENT   No
PARKING   No
BANQUET FACILITIES   No
DRESS   Casual
LIQUOR   Yes
WINE   Limited selection

Good food and the creative minds of the "Lettuce Entertain You" group make Fritz, That's It! a favorite hangout for the Northwestern college students and North Shore residents alike. The amusing menu lists items from fisshysoise (homemade fish soup) and Donald Duck (crisp duckling and cherry sauce) to their terrific salad bar, ranging from caviar to fresh fruit. While dining, you can view an unusual display of art by local artists. Some recommendations to keep in mind are the refreshing health juices, french-fried shrimp, Eggs Bon Vivant (an omelette with chicken livers, mushrooms, onions and cheese), and the selection of unusual sandwiches.

Waldorf Salad

Serves 4

1 large red apple	1 cup sour cream
3 stalks celery	1 tablespoon sugar
2 bananas	1 teaspoon cinnamon
Lemon juice	½ cup chopped walnuts
½ cup mayonnaise	

Wash and core apple. Wedge and cut into bite-size pieces. Dice celery and cut bananas into ⅛" medallions. Toss banana and apple with a little lemon juice. Blend mayonnaise and sour cream together with the sugar and cinnamon. Toss with the apples, bananas and celery. Place in serving dish and garnish top with chopped walnuts.

FU-LAMA GARDENS

ADDRESS   1233 East Golf Road, Schaumburg
TELEPHONE   882-1166
HOURS AND DAYS   Daily 11:30 A.M.–midnight
HOLIDAYS CLOSED   Labor Day, Thanksgiving, Christmas, New
        Year's Day
RESERVATIONS   Required
CREDIT CARDS   AE, DC, MC, VI
ENTERTAINMENT   Yes
PARKING   ample
BANQUET FACILITIES   Private room (20–100)
DRESS   Casual
LIQUOR   Yes
WINE   Limited selection

A delightful restaurant offering Polynesian, Szechwan, Indian and Japanese food on the dinner menu. Polynesian entertainment is featured in the lounge. The specialties recommended are the Pupu tray (an appetizer assortment served with flaming hibachi), Chicken Kalakala (chicken with mushrooms, bamboo shoots, water chestnuts, celery and cashews) flaming beef kebob, Shrimp Halakahiki (sweet and sour shrimp with pineapple), and the King Crab Martinique (King crab sautéed in light rum sauce, with tidbits of ham, served on a bed of rice).

Chicken Kalakala

Serves 4

2 pounds boneless chicken
breasts, cubed
4 teaspoons soy sauce
1 teaspoon sugar
¼ cup sherry
2 teaspoons cornstarch
Pinch each of ground
pepper, ginger, garlic
powder
½ teaspoon salt
½ cup oil

⅔ cup water chestnuts,
cubed
⅔ cup bamboo shoots
⅔ cup celery, diced
24 straw mushrooms
½ cup green pepper, chopped
½ cup onion, diced
⅔ cup chicken stock
1 cup toasted cashews
1 tablespoon pimientos,
diced

Marinate chicken in mixture of soy sauce, sugar, sherry, 1 teaspoon cornstarch, pepper, ginger, garlic and salt. Heat oil in pan and sauté chicken and vegetables. Simmer for 4 minutes. Add the stock and bring to a boil. Thicken with remaining teaspoon of cornstarch. Add cashews and the pimientos and mix well.

Wine suggestion: Wan Fu—soft French white wine

FULTON STREET FISHERY AND MARKET

ADDRESS   604 North Milwaukee Road, Wheeling
TELEPHONE   537-3930
HOURS AND DAYS   Lunch: Mon.–Fri. 11:30 A.M.–2:30 P.M.
Dinner: Mon.–Thurs. 5–11 P.M.; Fri., Sat. 5 P.M.–
midnight; Sun. 4:30–10:30 P.M.
HOLIDAYS CLOSED   None
RESERVATIONS   Yes
CREDIT CARDS   AE, MC, VI
ENTERTAINMENT   No
PARKING   Ample
BANQUET FACILITIES   No
DRESS   Casual
LIQUOR   Yes
WINE   Limited selection

Do you enjoy nostalgia? If so, then here's the place for you. It is great fun to see the small replicas of the old general store, hat shop, butcher shop, bread shop, garage and saloon. The food served is well above average. A salad bar and bread bar are wheeled to your table as is an a la carte ice cream bar filled with yummy sundae makings. When you first walk in, you'll see a blackboard announcing the special fresh fish of the day. Noteworthy are the chowder pot, Boston scrod, crab legs, scampi, broiled chicken and rib-eye steak. A wine cart is available and you have a chance to taste a variety of wines before you choose the one you want. A unique place with good food and unusual happenings.

Turbot à la Fulton

Serves 4

½ cup flour
2 pounds imported turbot
   fillets
3 ounces (6 tablespoons)
   clarified butter
2 4-ounce glasses Chablis
3 ripe tomatoes, diced

½ Spanish onion, diced fine
1 tablespoon fresh parsley,
   diced fine
Salt to taste
Pinch white pepper
½ garlic clove
Lemons

Flour the fillets. Place butter in pan, add fillets, wine, tomatoes, and onion and cook over medium heat for 5 minutes. Add parsley, salt, pepper and garlic; cover and simmer for another 5 minutes. Garnish with lemons.

Wine suggestion: Medium white Bordeaux or California wine

GAYLORD INDIA RESTAURANT

ADDRESS   678 North Clark Street
TELEPHONE   664-1700
HOURS AND DAYS   Lunch: Mon.–Fri. 11:30 A.M.–2 P.M.
          Dinner: Daily 5:30–10:30 P.M.
HOLIDAYS CLOSED   None
RESERVATIONS   Yes
CREDIT CARDS   All major cards
ENTERTAINMENT   No
PARKING   Yes
BANQUET FACILITIES   No
DRESS   Casual
LIQUOR   Yes
WINE   Limited selection

This is a nicely decorated Indian restaurant. The menu lists the standard Indian dishes plus the special Tandoor cooking. This is cooking in a special clay pot which keeps the juices in. The nan bread is great and perfect for soaking up the spicy sauces. The curry-flavored Mulligatawny Soup is good and different-tasting. The waiters are very friendly and responsive in explaining the menu. When you go there for the first time, try the combination plate so you get to taste a variety of foods.

Lamb Pasanda

Serves 2

2 ounces coriander seeds,
  ground
2 tablespoons white pepper
1 tablespoon turmeric
2 whole cloves
2 cardamom cloves (seeds),
  whole
4 ounces (½ cup) yogurt or
  sour cream
4 ounces (½ cup) light
  cream

1 pound lamb, cut into 1½"
  cubes
4 medium-size onions,
  chopped
½ cup shortening
  Salt, garlic and ginger to
  taste
1 cup water
1 hard-boiled egg, chopped

Mix coriander, pepper, turmeric, cloves and cardamom cloves (seeds) with yogurt (or sour cream) and light cream and marinate lamb 3 hours. Fry onion in shortening until golden brown. Add salt, garlic and ginger; fry for a few minutes. Add lamb and marinade. Fry until lamb turns light brown and the shortening separates from the gravy. Add water and cook till lamb is tender. Simmer on low fire for a few minutes. Garnish with egg. Serve with rice or chapati.

Wine suggestion: Dry red Bordeaux

GENE & GEORGETTI'S

ADDRESS   500 North Franklin Street
TELEPHONE   527-3718
HOURS AND DAYS   Mon.–Sat. 11:30 A.M.–midnight
HOLIDAYS CLOSED   July 4, Labor Day, Thanksgiving, Christmas,
        New Year's Day
RESERVATIONS   Yes
CREDIT CARDS   AE, DC
ENTERTAINMENT   No
PARKING   Free parking in lot behind restaurant
BANQUET FACILITIES   No
DRESS   Casual
LIQUOR   Yes
WINE   Limited, reasonable selection

    This popular restaurant is convenient to the downtown area. The quality of beef here is "out of sight." They buy the best and prepare it to perfection. The Limestone Salad is worth the extra price. A variety of Italian dishes adds spice to the menu. Service is delightful! You can never go wrong if you order any of their steaks. Some other enjoyable entrees are the Calf's Liver, Chicken Vesuvio, Veal Florentine, Shrimps De Jonge, and the Linguini with White Clam Sauce.

Chicken Vesuvio

Serves 2

1 2½-pound *frying chicken,*
quartered (separate legs,
thighs, wings, and breasts)
4 *ounces (½ cup) oil*

1 *potato, cubed*
1 *teaspoon chopped garlic*
1 *teaspoon oregano*
¼ *teaspoon salt*

Sauté the chicken in the oil until it is golden brown. Drain the excess oil and reserve it to cook the potato. Place the chicken into a casserole dish and cook for 15–20 minutes in a 350°–400° oven. While the chicken is cooking, use the excess oil to sauté the potato with the garlic, oregano and salt. Add browned potato and seasoned oil to chicken and cook for another 15 minutes. Put the chicken on a warm platter, pour the seasoned oil and potatoes over it and garnish with chopped parsley.

Wine suggestion: Medium red Italian wine

GIANNOTTI'S

ADDRESS   7711 West Roosevelt Road, Forest Park
TELEPHONE   366-1199
HOURS AND DAYS   Mon.–Sat. 4 P.M.–2 A.M.; Sun. 2–10 P.M.
HOLIDAYS CLOSED   Christmas, New Year's Day
RESERVATIONS   Yes
CREDIT CARDS   AE, CB, DC,
ENTERTAINMENT   No
PARKING   Attendant
BANQUET FACILITIES   No
DRESS   Casual
LIQUOR   Yes
WINE   Good selection

Giannotti's is a very well known Italian restaurant. The specialty of the house is food—at its finest! Giannotti's has received WBBM's award for the top Italian restaurant in Chicago four years in a row. In addition to many other awards, it has the American Express Recommended Gourmet Award, and the *Sun Times* has given Giannotti's the Five-Plate Award. You don't have to be Italian to like the food here—just have a hefty appetite. Some of our favorites are the Homemade Fettuccine Alfredo, Baked Rigatoni, Bragiole (rolled butt steak), Veal Saltimbocca (sliced veal cutlet stuffed with prosciutto and covered with baked cheese), Chicken a la Cacciatore (chicken sautéed in olive oil, white wine, fresh tomatoes, mushrooms) and the Calamari (baby squid).

Veal Picante

Serves 4

1½ pounds leg of veal, thinly
    sliced
    Flour for dredging
¼ cup olive oil

Juice of 1 lemon
Salt and pepper to taste
Pine nuts or parsley to
    taste, optional

Pound the veal lightly until very thin. Dredge with flour. Heat
the oil in skillet, add the veal and brown on both sides. Add the
lemon juice and season with salt and pepper. Sprinkle with pine
nuts or parsley, if desired.

Wine suggestion: Dry white Italian wine

GRASSFIELD'S INTERNATIONAL RESTAURANT

ADDRESS   6666 North Ridge Boulevard (and 1550 Waukegan Road, Glenview)

TELEPHONE   274-6666

HOURS AND DAYS   Daily 11 A.M.–4 A.M.

HOLIDAYS CLOSED   None

RESERVATIONS   Required Sat. nights and Sun. brunch

CREDIT CARDS   AE, MC

ENTERTAINMENT   Cabaret Lounge (Tues.–Sat.); Parisian Room (Wed.–Sun.)

PARKING   Attendant

BANQUET FACILITIES   25–110 in Victorian Room

DRESS   Casual to formal

LIQUOR   Yes

WINE   Good selection

The building which houses Grassfield's was first used as a coach house stop for travelers between Chicago and Milwaukee around 1867. Today the interior of this building has been remodeled into elegant dining rooms. Special promotions are planned on all holidays for your fun and enjoyment. Specialties of the house include Roast Duck Normandy (a whole crispy duckling stuffed with apple dressing and served with their special orange sauce), Baked Shrimp Denise (jumbo shrimp wrapped in bacon and served with wild rice), and Chicken de Jonghe (boneless chicken breasts baked in garlic butter sauce, herbs and wine). The reasonable prices include an appetizer, salad, potato or vegetable and beverage.

Duck a la Grassfield's

Serves 6

3 4-pound ducks
Salt and pepper
MSG (monosodium
  glutamate)
½ cup (1 stick) melted butter

Apple Dressing (see below)
Orange Sauce (see below)
1 orange, sliced
6 sprigs parsley

Sprinkle a bit of salt, pepper and MSG on ducks and brush each with the melted butter. Preheat oven to 350° and preheat roasting pan. Place ducks in the hot roasting pan and roast for 1½ hours, uncovered. Remove pan from oven and drain *all* fat and juices. Turn ducks over and return to oven at 450° for ½ hour. Remove from oven and let cool completely (until the next day, if you desire). Split ducks in half and fill cavities of each half with Apple Dressing; stuff tightly. Then place duck halves in roasting pan so that dressing is on bottom. Preheat oven to 350° and roast ducks for 25 minutes. Place half a duck on each serving plate, cover with Orange Sauce, garnish with sliced oranges and parsley, and serve.

APPLE DRESSING

12 slices stale white bread
12 slices whole wheat bread
6 ounces (¾ cup) canned
  chicken broth
½ cup chopped onion
1 cup chopped celery
¼ pound (1 stick) butter

1 8-ounce can sliced, plain
  (no sugar added) apples
2 tablespoons ground sage
2 tablespoons poultry
  seasoning
2 teaspoons MSG
1 teaspoon salt
¼ teaspoon pepper

Soak bread in chicken broth until soft. Saute onion and celery in butter until soft. Drain bread and add to skillet. Remove from heat and mix thoroughly. Add apples, sage, poultry seasoning, MSG, salt and pepper and mix well. It's now ready for stuffing into the ducks.

ORANGE SAUCE

8 ounces (1 cup) orange
  marmalade
8 ounces (1 cup) orange
  juice
½ teaspoon whole cloves
2 whole cinnamon sticks
2 tablespoons cornstarch
½ cup water

Combine marmalade, orange juice, cloves and cinnamon in a saucepan and bring to a boil. Dissolve cornstarch in water and stir in slowly, simmering until thickened. Remove cloves and cinnamon sticks before serving.

Wine suggestion: Medium white Alsatian or California wine

THE GREAT GRITZBE'S
FLYING FOOD SHOW

ADDRESS   21 East Chestnut Street
TELEPHONE   642-3460
HOURS AND DAYS   Mon.–Thurs. 11:30 A.M.–midnight; Fri., Sat.
      11:30 A.M.–1 A.M.; Sun. 10 A.M.–midnight (Sun. brunch
      10 A.M.–2:30 P.M.)
HOLIDAYS CLOSED   Thanksgiving, Christmas
RESERVATIONS   No
CREDIT CARDS   No
ENTERTAINMENT   No
PARKING   Reduced rate at 111 East Chestnut
BANQUET FACILITIES   No
DRESS   Casual
LIQUOR   Yes
WINE   Limited selection

Institution magazine selected this restaurant as one of the top ten in design for 1975. While waiting for your table, you may help yourself to the well-stocked cheese bar. The sandwiches and entrees consist of unusual, delicious combinations of food. They have a French mushroom and onion soup that's super and different in taste. The French Toast Connection (French toast stuffed with chicken salad and cheese and served with pineapple jam) sounds wild but tastes great. Their own baking company provides the countless tasty desserts displayed at the Help Yourself Dessert Bar.

Cheese Soup

Serves 12 or more

2 cups diced celery
1 medium diced onion
1 cup diced carrot
8 ounces (2 sticks) butter
2 quarts chicken stock
1 cup light cream
1 tablespoon celery seed

5 ounces (10 tablespoons) flour
2 pounds cheddar cheese, grated
Bacon, fried and crumbled
Chopped chives

Sauté celery, onion and carrot in 4 ounces (1 stick) butter. When onion has become translucent, add the chicken stock. Simmer for approximately 20 minutes. Add cream and celery seed; bring back to a boil. Make a roux with the flour and remaining butter, then stir into soup. Cook for another 10–15 minutes, stirring occasionally. Remove from the fire and stir in the cheese, a handful at a time. Serve immediately, garnished with crumbled bacon and chopped chives.

Wine suggestion: Dry white or mellow German Mosel wine

GREEK ISLANDS

ADDRESS   766 West Jackson Boulevard
TELEPHONE   782-9855
HOURS AND DAYS   Daily 11 A.M.–midnight
HOLIDAYS CLOSED   Thanksgiving, Christmas
RESERVATIONS   Suggested
CREDIT CARDS   AE, CB
ENTERTAINMENT   No
PARKING   Yes
BANQUET FACILITIES   No
DRESS   Casual
LIQUOR   Yes
WINE   Limited selection

The Greek music in the background sets your feet a-dancing. The cheerful blue and white checked tablecloths go along nicely with the hand-painted mural on the wall with scenes of water, a street and people in a bar. You can go over and see the chef working in the kitchen. The secret of the success of the gourmet cooking is that the chef is a partner in the restaurant. Authentic Greek dishes are offered with incredible sea bass, octopus, squid, codfish and shrimp. Everything is well prepared, and you are insured of good eating and a great time.

Nogatina

Serves 10–12

DOUGH

6 egg whites
½ pound almonds, grated

½ pound (1 cup) sugar
1 tablespoon cinnamon

Beat egg whites until stiff and glossy. Add almonds, sugar and cinnamon and beat a few minutes more. Lightly flour and grease 3 cake pans of the same size. Pour dough batter into each pan about ¼″ deep. Bake at 300° about 15 minutes or until brown. Take out of pans immediately before it gets sticky. Let the layers cool.

FILLING

24 ounces (3 cups) whole
   milk
6 egg yolks
½ cup sugar
½ cup flour

¼ cup cornstarch
1 teaspoon vanilla
½ pound (2 sticks) butter
   Whipped cream

Put milk and egg yolks in a pot and bring to a boil. Add sugar, flour, cornstarch and vanilla; stir until it boils. Add butter and stir; take pot off the stove and let cool. Put one meringue layer on a cake plate and put ½ of filling on it, repeat this procedure for the second layer, and on the third layer put the whipped cream. (This can be made in two layers instead of three.)

Wine suggestion: Sweet red Greek wine

HANS' BAVARIAN LODGE

ADDRESS   931 North Milwaukee Avenue, Wheeling
TELEPHONE   537-4141
HOURS AND DAYS   Mon., Wed.–Fri. 11:30 A.M.–10 P.M.;
      Sat. 4 P.M.–1 A.M.; Sun. noon–9 P.M.
HOLIDAYS CLOSED   Christmas Eve
RESERVATIONS   Suggested
CREDIT CARDS   MC, AE, DC, VI and house card
ENTERTAINMENT   Fri.–Sun.
PARKING   Yes
BANQUET FACILITIES   Up to 125 people
DRESS   Casual
LIQUOR   Yes
WINE   Limited selection

This authentic German restaurant is warm and atmospheric with many handsomely decorated rooms. The food is plentiful and nicely done. The delectable highlights are the German pot roast, duck and the Wiener Schnitzel a la Holstein. The German theme continues with the presence of various beer steins and the peasant costumes of the waitresses. A must is Hans' and Paula's annual Oktoberfest, for lots of fun, good food and lively entertainment.

Roast Long Island Duckling a la Maison

Serves 6

3 4-pound ducklings	¼ apple, chopped
Salt and pepper	¼ onion, chopped
Thyme or rosemary leaves	

Place ducks on rack in roasting pan. Add 1″ water to bottom of pan. Season the duck cavities with salt, pepper, and thyme or rosemary to taste. Divide apple and onion into three parts and place in cavities with seasonings. Roast ducks in oven at 400°–425° for 2 hours and 10 minutes. Keep covered for the first hour only. Baste ducks during cooking time with the water and meat drippings from bottom of pan.

DUXELLES
(To be served as side dish with ducklings)

6 cups rice	¼ pound fresh mushrooms
4 tablespoons butter	Salt, pepper and nutmeg
½ medium onion, finely	to taste
chopped	¼ pound sliced blanched
2 shallots, finely chopped	almonds

Cook rice in water with 1 tablespoon butter and onion until done (follow package directions). Melt 2 tablespoons butter in pan and sauté shallots, mushrooms and seasonings. (Liver or giblets from ducklings may be added here if desired.) Stir over a high heat for 4–5 minutes; this will result in a paste-like texture. Add cooked rice to the duxelle. Sauté almonds in 1 tablespoon butter. Mix together with rice mixture.

FRESH VEGETABLE MARKET
(To be served as side dish with ducklings and Duxelle)

1 *head of cauliflower*
1 *pint milk*
½ *pound green beans*
½ *pound asparagus*
¼ *pound Belgian carrots*
½ *pound June peas*
1¾ *sticks butter*
3 *tomatoes*
Salt and pepper
½ *cup bread crumbs*
2 *hard boiled eggs, chopped*
Parsley, chopped

Boil whole cauliflower in 1 pint milk and salted water to cover. Cook green beans, asparagus, carrots and peas in separate saucepans. Add 2 tablespoons of butter and a little water to each pan. Core tomatoes and bake in 375° oven for 10–12 minutes. Season all vegetables with salt and pepper to taste. After vegetables are cooked, strain. Arrange on platter with cauliflower in center and vegetables in mounds around the cauliflower. Melt remaining ¾ stick (6 tablespoons) butter in saucepan, add bread crumbs and cook to a golden brown. Add the eggs, mix and pour over the cauliflower. Make sure that all the vegetables are good and hot.
Wine suggestion: Medium white German wine

HOMESTEAD

ADDRESS   12126 South Vincennes Street, Blue Island
TELEPHONE   385-2570
HOURS AND DAYS   Tues.–Thurs. 4:30 P.M.–12:30 A.M.;
        Fri., Sat. 4:30 P.M.–1:30 A.M.;
        Sun. 1–10:30 P.M.
HOLIDAYS CLOSED   December 12–December 26
RESERVATIONS   No
CREDIT CARDS   AE
ENTERTAINMENT   No
PARKING   Adjacent parking lot
BANQUET FACILITIES   Weekdays—available to 100 people
DRESS   Casual
LIQUOR   Yes
WINE   Limited selection

This restaurant started out as a one-room tavern and now has three main dining rooms and a bar. It has been in business for over fifty years in the same location, and the present owners have owned it for the last ten years. The specialty of the house is the delicious barbecued back ribs, smoked and cooked on a real hickory log pit. It's an informal place with comfortable settings and pleasant service.

Banana Bread

1 *loaf*

3 *cups flour*
¾ *cup sugar*
1 *teaspoon salt*
2 *teaspoons baking powder*
1 *teaspoon baking soda*
1¼ *cups mashed ripe bananas*

2 *eggs*
½ *cup buttermilk*
⅓ *cup melted shortening*
1 *teaspoon grated lemon peel*
¾ *cup chopped nuts*

Sift flour, sugar, salt, baking powder and baking soda together. Add remaining ingredients and mix thoroughly. Pour into greased loaf pan and let stand 20 minutes. Bake at 325° for an hour.

HOTSPUR'S

ADDRESS   7 West Division Street
TELEPHONE   787-8141
HOURS AND DAYS   Lunch: Mon.–Sat. 11:30 A.M.–3 P.M.
        Brunch: Sat., Sun. 10 A.M.–3 P.M.
        Dinner: Mon.–Thurs. 5 P.M.–midnight; Fri. 5 P.M.–
            1 A.M.; Sat., Sun. 3 P.M.–midnight
HOLIDAYS CLOSED   Christmas Eve
RESERVATIONS   Parties over 6
CREDIT CARDS   AE, MC, VI
ENTERTAINMENT   No
PARKING   No
BANQUET FACILITIES   No
DRESS   Casual
LIQUOR   Yes—special drink menu
WINE   Good selection

A tastefully decorated restaurant, Hotspur's is clean and bright with lots of lovely greenery, which presents an exciting atmosphere, and a creative menu which provides dishes you'll like. The ribs, omelets, hamburgers and salads are delightfully good. Service is industrious and aims to please. If you like typical American food presented in a light and airy environment, this is the place for you.

Eggs Vegetarian

Serves 2

½ cup spinach (fresh, if
  possible; frozen if
  necessary)
Cheese Sauce (see below)

1 English muffin, toasted
2 artichoke hearts
2 poached eggs
  Hollandaise Sauce

If using fresh spinach, rinse thoroughly. Chop spinach leaves
into 1" squares. Cook fresh spinach (with just the water that
clings to leaves) until tender; follow package directions for frozen spinach. Strain spinach and mix with cheese sauce. Place
half of spinach mixture on each half of the English muffin, then
an artichoke heart, then a poached egg. Top with Hollandaise
Sauce.

CHEESE SAUCE

1 cup milk
2 tablespoons butter
2 tablespoons flour

¼ teaspoon salt
⅛ teaspoon pepper
½ cup grated cheddar cheese

Scald the milk. Melt the butter in a saucepan over low heat or in
a double boiler. Add flour, stirring constantly, then stir in the
hot milk. Add salt and pepper and stir until mixture thickens.
Add cheese. If lumpy, beat well with rotary beater.
Wine suggestion: Medium white German wine

HY'S OF CHICAGO

ADDRESS   100 East Walton Street
TELEPHONE   649-9555
HOURS AND DAYS   Lunch: Mon.–Fri. 11:30 A.M.–2:30 P.M.
     Dinner: Daily 5:30 P.M.–midnight
HOLIDAYS CLOSED   Easter, Memorial Day, Thanksgiving,
     Christmas, New Year's Day
RESERVATIONS   Necessary weekends
CREDIT CARDS   AE, CB, DC, MC, VI
ENTERTAINMENT   Piano bar
PARKING   Public lot
BANQUET FACILITIES   No
DRESS   Jacket
LIQUOR   Yes
WINE   Good selection

If atmosphere is high on your preference list, then this is the place for you. Upon entering you'll find a library of books lining the walls leading into the main dining room. The large bar area provides comfortable seating and soothing piano music. They serve well prepared meats and fish. For an evening of elegance and sophistication, you'll enjoy dining here. We recommend starting with the Escargots (snails in garlic butter) or the Oysters Rockefeller (oysters, spinach, cream sauce); the most satisfying entrees are the steaks, rack of lamb, sweetbreads, trout stuffed with seafood and the Beef Wellington (filet wrapped in a pastry crust).

Stuffed Trout

Serves 1

2½ ounces King crabmeat
 1 ounce bay shrimps, peeled
 and deveined
 ¼ cup chopped mushrooms
 4 tablespoons butter
 1 shot glass (or 2
 tablespoons) white wine

½ cup medium cream sauce
 Salt and pepper
 1 10-ounce trout, boned
 1 egg white, beaten lightly
 ¼ cup flour

Sauté the crabmeat and shrimps with the mushrooms in 2 table-spoons butter. Add the white wine and cream sauce. Season all to taste. Dip boneless trout in egg white and then in the flour. Sauté in 2 tablespoons hot butter on both sides; when done, fill with stuffing and serve.

Wine suggestion: Dry white California wine

ICHIBAN OF CHICAGO

ADDRESS   3155 North Broadway Avenue
TELEPHONE   935-3636
HOURS AND DAYS   Mon.–Thurs. 5–10:30 P.M.;
          Fri., Sat. 5–11:30 P.M.;
          Sun. 4–9 P.M.
HOLIDAYS CLOSED   None
RESERVATIONS   Weekends only
CREDIT CARDS   AE, MC
ENTERTAINMENT   No
PARKING   No
BANQUET FACILITIES   No
DRESS   Casual
LIQUOR   Yes
WINE   Limited house wines

Ichiban's natural setting of wood and rice-paper construction has a teahouse-like interior. The seating is an informal arrangement of butcher-block tables and booths. The Japanese cuisine is exceptionally flavorful. Treasure Pleasure, a mixed sea food tempura, was especially good. The hot noodle soup with onions and the beef teriyaki were also very tasty.

Teriyaki Sauce

Serves 4

3 ounces (6 tablespoons) soy
 sauce
1 ounce (2 tablespoons)
 Mirin (sweet saki)
3 ounces (6 tablespoons)
 water

2 ounces (¼ cup) sugar
1 slice each ginger, garlic,
 lemon
2 tablespoons cornstarch
 mixed with ¼ cup water

Boil all ingredients except cornstarch mixture; add cornstarch
and boil again. Use as a marinade to make Pork, Chicken, Fish
or Beef Teriyaki.

IGNATZ AND MARY'S GROVE INN

ADDRESS   3555 Milwaukee Avenue (Milwaukee and Lake
    Avenues), Northbrook
TELEPHONE   824-7141
HOURS AND DAYS   Mon., Wed.–Fri. 11 A.M.–10:30 P.M.;
    Sat. 11 A.M.–11:30 P.M.;
    Sun. 11:30 A.M.–9:30 P.M.
HOLIDAYS CLOSED   Christmas
RESERVATIONS   Necessary for 9 or more only
CREDIT CARDS   AE, DC, MC
ENTERTAINMENT   Organist (Fri.–Sun.)
PARKING   Yes
BANQUET FACILITIES   Small groups
DRESS   Casual
LIQUOR   Yes
WINE   Good selection

The Grove Inn has been in the same location for almost a hundred years. The owners have changed several times, but in 1945 the present owners, Ignatz and Mary, took over and have continued to improve the food and service ever since. Highlights are the Schlachtfest in October and a wild game dinner party in January. Specialties are roast duck and sauerbraten with homemade red cabbage. They serve delicious homemade pies and strudel.

Sauerbraten, Dumplings and Gravy

Serves 15

1 *heaping tablespoon*
  pickling spices

6 *pounds beef round, cut in*
  3 long pieces

1 *cup cider vinegar*
1 *cup wine vinegar*
1 *quart warm water*
1 *medium onion, cut up*

1 *large carrot, cut up*
2 *stalks celery, cut up*
1 *clove garlic, cut up*

Heat the spices in 2 cups water to boiling and let cool. Put meat in a large pot and add spices with their water and all remaining ingredients; let stand for 5 days in refrigerator, turning every day. To roast: Put in roasting pan to fit size of meat. Season with salt and pepper and add vegetables from brine. Cover roasting pan and roast at 375° for 2½ hours or until done. Serve with Dumplings and Gravy.

DUMPLINGS

1 *cup flour*
1 *teaspoon baking powder*
¼ *teaspoon salt*
1 *egg*

1 *tablespoon butter*
Pinch parsley
⅓ *cup milk*

Mix dry ingredients, then add remaining ingredients; mix all together. Drop by spoonfuls into a pot of salted (1 tablespoon) boiling water and boil, covered, for 8 minutes.

GRAVY

Boil all meat drippings and brine, thicken with ¼ cup flour and add ½ cup sour cream and ¼ cup Burgundy. Whip up, strain and serve.

Wine suggestion: Full-bodied white German wine

ILE DE FRANCE

ADDRESS   1177 North Elston Avenue
TELEPHONE   278-0114
HOURS AND DAYS   Lunch: Wed.–Sat. 11:30 A.M.–3 P.M.
        Dinner: Mon.–Sat. 6–11 P.M.
HOLIDAYS CLOSED   All major holidays
RESERVATIONS   Suggested
CREDIT CARDS   AE
ENTERTAINMENT   No
PARKING   Street
BANQUET FACILITIES   No
DRESS   Casual
LIQUOR   Yes
WINE   Good selection

Overlooking the Chicago River, Ile de France gives the feeling of a seaside cafe. The combination of the small, intimate dining room and the fireplace, brightly lit during the winter months, creates a peaceful, romantic atmosphere. The baked escargots and Scampi Sauté Provençale are both excellent for your first course. Lobster Thermidor, Dover Sole Balmoral (sautéed in butter with smoked salmon and scampi), or Veal Normande are recommended for delicious entrees.

Entrecôte Marchand de Vin

Serves 4

Marrow from beef bone
5 shallots, minced
⅔ cup red wine

½ cup beef stock or bouillon
1 2-pound sirloin steak
2 tablespoons oil

Split bone with a cleaver to expose the marrow. Remove a 4″ piece of marrow and dice it. In a saucepan, combine shallots, wine, beef stock or bouillon and marrow. Simmer for 10 minutes, until liquid has reduced. In a frying pan, sauté steak in oil. When steak has reached the desired doneness, place on platter and pour sauce over it. Serve immediately.

Wine suggestion: Dry red Bordeaux, Burgundy or California wine

THE INDIAN TRAIL

ADDRESS   507 Chestnut Street, Winnetka
TELEPHONE   446-1703
HOURS AND DAYS   Tues.–Sat. 11:30 A.M.–2:30 P.M., 4:30–8 P.M.;
        Sun. 11:30 A.M.–7:30 P.M.
HOLIDAYS CLOSED   Christmas
RESERVATIONS   No
CREDIT CARDS   MC, VI
ENTERTAINMENT   No
PARKING   No
BANQUET FACILITIES   No
DRESS   Casual—but no tennis clothes
LIQUOR   No—bring your own
WINE   Bring your own

Excellent service and well-prepared dinners make this restaurant run by the Klingman family a great place for comfortable and friendly dining. The prices are lower Tuesday through Friday. The menu changes daily, and they have their own bake shop preparing all the pies, cakes, tarts and rolls. Everything is fresh tasting and served nicely. We recommend the fried chicken, whitefish, veal cutlet, and roast leg of lamb; they are all consistently good.

Glazed Chicken Liver Pâté

1 *party mold*

1 *cup chicken liver pâté (or see recipe for substitute)*
1 *10½-ounce can condensed beef consommé*
½ *cup water*
1 *bay leaf*
1 *teaspoon salt and dash of pepper*

1 *3-ounce package lemon-flavored gelatin*
2 *tablespoons dry sauterne*
1 *tablespoon lemon juice*
1 *tablespoon tarragon vinegar*
1 *3-ounce jar stuffed olives, thinly sliced*
2 *hard-boiled eggs, sliced*

If chicken liver pâté is not available, cook about ¾ pound of chicken livers in simmering salted water or chicken stock until tender. Cool. Put livers through the fine knife of a food chopper 2 or 3 times. Combine with enough butter to make a smooth paste and season thoroughly with salt, onion juice, garlic salt and pepper.

Press pâté into a small buttered mold and chill. Combine consommé, water, bay leaf, salt and pepper in a small saucepan. Cover and simmer 5 minutes. Remove bay leaf and dissolve gelatin in hot liquid. Add sauterne, lemon juice and vinegar and chill until syrupy. Unmold pâté and garnish with olives and egg slices, if desired. Pour a thin layer of gelatin over the top and chill until the gelatin is almost firm. Pour over a second layer of gelatin and chill until almost firm, then add a third layer and chill until set.

Wine suggestion: Dry white Bordeaux or California wine

IRELAND'S

ADDRESS   500 North LaSalle Street
TELEPHONE   337-2020
HOURS AND DAYS   Lunch: Mon.–Fri. 11 A.M.–5 P.M.
           Dinner: Mon.–Sat. 5 P.M.–midnight; Sun. 2–10 P.M.
HOLIDAYS CLOSED   Thanksgiving, Christmas Eve, Christmas
RESERVATIONS   Suggested
CREDIT CARDS   AE, CB, DC, MC, VI
ENTERTAINMENT   No
PARKING   After 5 P.M.
BANQUET FACILITIES   No
DRESS   Casual
LIQUOR   Yes
WINE   Limited selection

Seafood comes first here, with an abundant selection of fresh fish. Landlubbers don't have to panic, as they have small but tasty choices of steak or broiled chicken. Everyone can enjoy the complete circular salad bar, which is well stocked with fresh fruits and vegetables. We had a very enjoyable meal which consisted of clam chowder, shrimp scampi, and the Crab Louis Salad. Also available is a meal for two in a bucket, called Ireland's Bucket. It consists of two lobsters, crab, shrimp, mussels, corn on the cob and redskins, with a price of $11.75 per person. Two seafood lovers will certainly find this choice a delightful treat.

Shrimp Scampi

Serves 4

12 *large shrimp scampi (6"–8"*
   shrimp), peeled and
   deveined
 8 *tablespoons of butter*

Garlic and parsley,
   chopped
16 *large mushrooms, chopped*
 1½ *cups dry white wine*

Heat small frying pan for approximately 60 seconds. Drop in shrimp and turn immediately (object is to sear both sides only). Add butter, garlic, parsley, mushrooms and white wine. Cook for approximately 4 to 6 minutes. Place shrimp on plate and cover with sauce. Garnish with lemon wedge and parsley sprig.

Wine suggestion: Dry white Burgundy

ITALIAN VILLAGE (THE FLORENTINE ROOM)

ADDRESS 71 West Monroe Street
TELEPHONE 332-7005
HOURS AND DAYS Lunch: Mon.–Fri. 11:30 A.M.–2 P.M.
        Dinner: Mon.–Fri. 5–10 P.M.; Sat. 5 P.M.–midnight
HOLIDAYS CLOSED All major holidays
RESERVATIONS Yes
CREDIT CARDS AE, DC
ENTERTAINMENT Strolling musicians
PARKING Valet or free parking at 215 West Monroe (Central
        National Garage)
BANQUET FACILITIES No
DRESS Semi-casual
LIQUOR Yes
WINE Good selection

Italian Village consists of three separate restaurants—La Cantina, with Italian and Continental cuisine; The Village, simulating an Italian town and offering casual Italian food; and The Florentine Room, elegant and sophisticated, specializing in Northern Italian cuisine. The Florentine Room has earned recognition from *Holiday* magazine and was cited by the Chicago *Tribune* as the "best Italian restaurant in Chicago." They offer a large selection of excellent entrees and the menu suggests the wine appropriate for each dish. It's almost impossible to go wrong with anything you may order within the Italian Village. We ordered the Italian dishes and found the fettuccine and cannelloni superb. Their menu is by no means only Italian, but offers a wide range of interesting dishes.

Petti di Pollo alla Strozzi

Serves 2

2 *boneless chicken breasts*	*Fontina or mozzarella*
Flour	*cheese*
Butter	½ *cup Verdicchio white wine*
2 *mushrooms*	½ *cup chicken stock*
Salt and pepper	1 *tablespoon brandy*

Remove skin from chicken breasts and flatten with the side of a cleaver. Dredge lightly with flour and cook slowly in hot butter for 5 or 6 minutes on each side. Remove them to a shallow broiler pan; season with salt and pepper. Arrange on each breast a slice of cheese and 1 mushroom which has been sliced and simmered in butter. Stir the wine, chicken stock and brandy into the juices remaining in the frying pan. Simmer for 10 minutes, or until the liquid is reduced and has thickened slightly. Add salt and pepper if necessary. Stir in a lump of butter at the end. Place chicken breasts under a hot broiler just long enough to melt the cheese and serve at once. Pass sauce separately.

Wine suggestion: Dry white Italian wine

JASAND'S

ADDRESS   720 North Rush Street
TELEPHONE   787-2701
HOURS AND DAYS   Lunch: Mon.–Sat. 11:30 A.M.–4:30 P.M.
          Dinner: Mon.–Sat. 5–11:30 P.M.; Sun. 4:30–10:30 P.M.
HOLIDAYS CLOSED   All major holidays
RESERVATIONS   Yes, for 4 or more
CREDIT CARDS   MC, VI
ENTERTAINMENT   No
PARKING   City lot across the street
BANQUET FACILITIES   No
DRESS   Casual
LIQUOR   Yes
WINE   Limited selection

The housing of Jasand's is an elegant four-story mansion; however, when you enter you'll see an exciting, informal decor. The bar is shaped like a piano with black and white piano keys leading up to it. Many unusual drinks are served here. Casseroles, salads, sandwiches and omelettes are the main items offered. The casseroles are made up of interesting combinations and include a beef stroganoff casserole, a seafood casserole and a delightful chicken casserole. The chicken is baked in a sauce of coconut and orange and served over wild rice. The omelettes are also good and are served with coffeecakes and fruit.

Chicken Coconage

Serves 10

Butter
2 ounces (4 tablespoons)
  flour
3 cups orange juice
1 6-ounce can of pure
  coconut cream
2–3 tablespoons sugar
6 tablespoons orange liqueur
  (Grand Marnier)
10 8-ounce chicken breasts

Salt and pepper
Long-grain wild rice mix
1 small can of whole
  cranberry sauce
1 small can of Mandarin
  oranges
1 small can of shredded
  coconut
1 orange, sliced

Cook 4 tablespoons butter and flour over low heat. Do not brown. In another pan, bring the orange juice, coconut cream, sugar and liqueur to a boil. Thicken with the flour mixture. Sauté skinned chicken breasts in butter, seasoned with salt and pepper, until ¾ cooked. Remove and cool. Divide wild rice, cooked according to package, among 10 individual casseroles. Put a portion of cranberry sauce in middle of rice. Place chicken on top. Garnish with Mandarin orange sections. Cover each portion with orange-coconut sauce and bake for 15 minutes at 350°. Garnish with coconut and orange slices.

Wine suggestion: California or French Pinot Chardonnay or Spanish or Chilean dry white wine

JONATHAN LIVINGSTON SEAFOOD

ADDRESS   5419 North Sheridan Road
TELEPHONE   878-1846
HOURS AND DAYS   Mon.–Thurs. 11:30 A.M.–midnight; Fri., Sat.
    11:30 A.M.–1 A.M.; Sun. 10 A.M.–midnight
HOLIDAYS CLOSED   Thanksgiving, Christmas
RESERVATIONS   On a limited basis
CREDIT CARDS   No
ENTERTAINMENT   No
PARKING   Reduced rate at Edgewater Plaza parking lot
BANQUET FACILITIES   No
DRESS   Casual
LIQUOR   Yes
WINE   Limited selection

Seafood, seafood and more seafood is served at this
beautifully decorated restaurant. The white structural curves are
accented with gray tones. The dominant colors come from the
large, scrumptious seafood bar filled with the most elaborate ar-
ray imaginable. The extensive menu offers seafood entrees of
every type. Two entrees that we strongly recommend are the
Lobster Tail de Jonghe and the Whitefish Jonathan's (Lake Superior whitefish broiled with onions and topped with toasted sesame seeds). For those people not in a seafood mood, an ade-
quate selection is available. Their three nightly specials are
offered from the freshest fish available that day. Of course, the
seafood is carried on into the house dressing, which is anchovy,
but it comes to a halt at dessert time. Their chocolate crepe pie
and banana eclairs are delicious.

Clam Chowder

Serves 6

1 large potato, peeled
1 medium onion
1 medium carrot
12 ounces (3 sticks) butter
1 quart clam juice
1 bay leaf
Pinch of thyme

6 ounces chopped clams
1 cup heavy cream
5 ounces (½ cup plus 2 tablespoons) flour
Salt, white pepper and nutmeg

Cut potato, onion and carrot into large dice. Sauté in 8 ounces (2 sticks) butter until onions are translucent. Pour in clam juice and simmer until potatoes are soft. Add the bay leaf and thyme. Then add the chopped clams and the heavy cream. Melt the remaining butter, add the flour and cook to a smooth roux. When soup comes to a rolling boil, add the roux bit by bit until soup is thick enough to coat a spoon. Season to taste. Simmer another 5 minutes, then serve.

Wine suggestion: Portuguese Vinho Verde

JOVAN

ADDRESS   16 East Huron Street
TELEPHONE   944-7766
HOURS AND DAYS   Lunch: Mon.–Fri. noon–3 P.M.
           Dinner: Mon.–Sat. 6–10 P.M.
HOLIDAYS CLOSED   All major holidays
RESERVATIONS   Preferred
CREDIT CARDS   AE, DC
ENTERTAINMENT   No
PARKING   Valet
BANQUET FACILITIES   No
DRESS   Jacket
LIQUOR   Yes
WINE   Extensive selection

Jovan is located in a three-story brownstone with an ambiance that's cheerful and intimate. They received a *Holiday* Award in 1976 and four stars from the Mobil Guide in 1976. The owner, Jovan Trboyevic, shops daily for the freshest foods and plans his daily specialties according to what's available. Among our favorites are the salmon mousse pâté, loin lamb chops and the Sautéed Veal "Marengo." Whether or not you're a dessert eater, it's a must to try their fantastic Grand Marnier Soufflé. It's a perfect ending to a delightful meal.

Coquilles St. Jacques "Provençale"

Serves 6

4 ounces (½ cup) olive oil
2 pounds fresh bay scallops
Flour
¼ pound (1 stick) fresh
unsalted butter
6 shallots, chopped
2 tablespoons chopped
parsley

4 tomatoes, peeled and
diced
4 cloves garlic, chopped
Dash of Pernod
¾ cup white wine
Salt and pepper

Bring olive oil to high heat in a frying skillet. Roll scallops lightly in flour and add to oil. Sauté quickly until golden brown. Remove from frying pan and put aside. Heat butter in saucepan and sauté shallots. Stir. Add parsley, tomatoes and garlic, stirring for a couple of minutes, until nicely sautéed. Add Pernod and white wine. Let reduce for a little while, then add scallops, salt and pepper. Simmer for a minute before serving. Garnish with chopped parsley, tomato wedges and garlic croutons.

Wine suggestion: Dry white Loire or California wine

KAHALA TERRACE

ADDRESS   3065 Dundee Road, Northbrook
TELEPHONE   272-5100
HOURS AND DAYS   Mon.–Thurs. 11:30 A.M.–10 P.M.; Fri. 11:30
          A.M.–11 P.M.; Sat. 5–11 P.M.; Sun. 5–10 P.M.
HOLIDAYS CLOSED   Labor Day, Thanksgiving, Christmas
RESERVATIONS   No
CREDIT CARDS   AE, MC
ENTERTAINMENT   No
PARKING   Yes
BANQUET FACILITIES   No
DRESS   Casual
LIQUOR   Yes
WINE   Limited selection

Here's a lovely Polynesian restaurant found in a small shopping center. There are unusual appetizers for nibbling and the food is good. The Puu Puu Platter consists of egg rolls, fried shrimp, skewered marinated beef, crab in won ton and fried chicken with pineapple. The Cantonese and Polynesian buffet is complete and well prepared. Also tasty are the pepper steak, almond duck, shrimp in lobster sauce, chicken pineapple, and the Kahala Beef (beef and vegetables in oyster sauce). The service is attentive and nice.

Kahala Beef

Serves 2

2 tablespoons cottonseed oil
7 ounces beef tenderloin
2½ ounces bok toi (Chinese cabbage), cut in 1" chunks
1 dozen Chinese pea pods; remove string from side and cut in half
1 dozen water chestnuts, sliced thin
1 dozen bamboo shoots

10 fresh mushrooms, sliced
1 small stalk, top and bottom broccoli, sliced thin
10 canned or bottled button mushrooms
1 tablespoon bottled oyster sauce
½ tablespoon cornstarch

Use either a wok or a heavy frying pan. Put cottonseed oil in pan and let it get very hot. Put the remaining ingredients except cornstarch in pan and stir-fry for 2–3 minutes or until the meat is browned. Add cornstarch to thicken sauce. Serve with rice.
Wine suggestion: Pinot Noir or other full-bodied red Burgundy

KING'S WHARF

ADDRESS   Lincolnshire Marriott Resort, Lincolnshire
TELEPHONE   634-0100
HOURS AND DAYS   Lunch: Mon.–Sat. 11:30 A.M.–2:30 P.M.
        Dinner: Mon.–Fri. 5:30–11 P.M.; Sat. 6 P.M.–12:30 A.M.;
            Sun. 5–10 P.M.
HOLIDAYS CLOSED   None
RESERVATIONS   Recommended
CREDIT CARDS   All major cards
ENTERTAINMENT   Yes
PARKING   Yes
BANQUET FACILITIES   Yes
DRESS   Jacket
LIQUOR   Yes
WINE   Good selection

This intimate restaurant and cocktail lounge is on eight levels and is decorated to resemble an 18th-century sailing vessel. The nautical theme is done in rich reds and golds. Two excellent entrees are the Veal Oscar (veal with crabmeat and asparagus topped with a fabulous Hollandaise sauce), and the Steak and Leg, a combo of King crab legs and filet mignon. The hot fudge sundae is fantastic. The Lincolnshire Marriott Resort also has a dinner-theater package at their other restaurant, The Chaparral. You receive a delicious prime rib of beef dinner and a stimulating night of theater at Drury Lane North.

Oysters J.W.

Serves 6

2 tablespoons butter
2 tablespoons flour
2¼ cups fish stock (or see
   recipe for substitute)
3 tablespoons minced
   shallots, or whites of green
   onions, or pearl onions or
   onions
½ clove garlic
3 tablespoons butter
3 medium mushrooms,
   chopped

⅔ cup crabmeat, shredded
3 tablespoons white wine
2 tablespoons lemon juice
2 tablespoons parsley,
   minced
¼ teaspoon salt
⅛ teaspoon pepper
36 oysters and half shells
   Rock salt
6 tablespoons grated
   Parmesan cheese

First make the velouté (rich white sauce for fish): Melt butter in saucepan, stir in flour. Cook over low heat, stirring constantly. Mix in fish stock or substitute. (You may substitute for the fish stock an equal amount of canned clam juice or chicken stock, or broth made by cooking 6 oysters in 3 cups water about 15 minutes.) Cook over low heat for 15 minutes. Reserve 1½ cups and set aside. Next sauté shallots and garlic in butter. Do not brown. Add mushrooms, cook a minute, then add crabmeat, wine and lemon juice. Simmer 2–3 minutes. Stir in parsley, velouté sauce (still reserving 1½ cups), salt and pepper. Cool. Shuck oysters. Place 36 half shells firmly in a shallow baking pan filled with a layer of rock salt. In each half shell place 1 teaspoon of reserved velouté sauce. Lay an oyster atop each half shell, top with crab mixture, then more velouté sauce. Sprinkle with Parmesan cheese. Bake 10 minutes at 450°. Serve immediately.
Wine: Dry white Burgundy, Bordeaux, or California wine

KLAS

ADDRESS   5734 Cermak Road, Cicero
TELEPHONE   652-0795; Chicago number 242-4100
HOURS AND DAYS   Tues.–Fri. and Sun. 11:30 A.M.–10 P.M.; Sat.
      11:30 A.M.–1 A.M.
HOLIDAYS CLOSED   Labor Day
RESERVATIONS   Not necessary
CREDIT CARDS   AE, DC
ENTERTAINMENT   No
PARKING   Yes
BANQUET FACILITIES   Up to 300
DRESS   Casual
LIQUOR   Yes
WINE   Limited selection

A real treat to experience is the Czechoslovakian as well as the Continental cuisine served at Klas. The hand-carved fixtures and cut-crystal glassware lend an air of authenticity to the decor. The Long Island duck is served with a side dish of sauerkraut and a dumpling. The chef's specials include beef goulash with dumplings, and sauerbraten with venison gravy and a dumpling. Both are tasty treats. For dessert, the homemade apple strudel and assorted kolachy are delicious.

Pickled Beef

Serves 4

2–3 pounds beef tenderloin (or
   eye of round)
   Salt and pepper
3 ounces bacon, cut into
   small strips (lardons)
8 ounces (1 cup) vegetables
   (carrot, celery root, parsley
   root), cut up into small
   pieces
1 large onion, sliced
8 bay leaves

Thyme
6 whole allspice
2 cups vinegar
4 ounces (1 stick) butter
2 tablespoons flour
   Juice from 3 lemons
8 ounces (1 cup) sour cream
2 cups half and half (or
   milk)
   Salt, pepper, sugar
   (optional)

The day before you want to serve: Trim the meat; salt and pepper it; make 1″ deep holes all around and fill with bacon. Place meat in flameproof, ovenproof pot; spread cut-up vegetables, onion, bay leaves, thyme and allspice over top and pour vinegar over. Let marinate overnight.

Next day, add butter and simmer until half of liquid is gone. Then put it in the oven (325°) for 2–2½ hours, until meat is tender, liquid evaporated, and vegetables brown. During this time turn meat over a few times and pour pan juices over it. Remove meat from pan. Sprinkle vegetables in pan with flour and brown slowly. Add 2 cups water and lemon juice and let it boil a short time. Then pour it through a sieve, pressing vegetables through sieve with a spoon; add sour cream and half and half (or milk) and boil for a few minutes. Taste and add salt and pepper if necessary. If too sour, add sugar (1–2 tablespoons). Slice meat and put into the gravy.

Drink suggestion: German beer

KON-TIKI PORTS

ADDRESS   505 North Michigan Avenue (Sheraton-Chicago
    Hotel)
TELEPHONE   527-4286
HOURS AND DAYS   Mon.–Thurs. 11:30 A.M.–11:30 P.M.;
    Fri., Sat. 11:30 A.M.–12:30 A.M.; Sun. 4–11:30 P.M.
    Cocktails daily until 1:30 A.M.
HOLIDAYS CLOSED   Thanksgiving, Christmas, New Year's Day
RESERVATIONS   Suggested
CREDIT CARDS   All major cards
ENTERTAINMENT   No
PARKING   On premises
BANQUET FACILITIES   No
DRESS   Jacket preferred
LIQUOR   Yes
WINE   Good selection

Kon-Tiki has a South-Seas atmosphere; the decor de-
picts five different ports of call. It offers extensive selections of
Polynesian and American specialties. There are more than 70
exotic drinks available from Singapore Joe's Waterfront Tavern.
Opened in 1962, Kon-Tiki Ports has since received many major
restaurant awards and continues to maintain its high standard of
quality. Begin your meal with an assortment of their flavorful
appetizers. The waiters are very helpful in suggesting entrees
from their many selections. The Beef Bing Chan and Pork Canton (a sweet and sour dish), are both delicious. The menu offers
combination ideas for entrees. These complete dinners include
appetizers to dessert and are priced within a range of $9.50 to
$11.75 per person.

Chicken Coral Sea

Serves 4

4 tablespoons peanut oil
½ teaspoon salt
12 ounces white chicken
   meat, diced
2 cups bamboo shoots, diced
2 cups water chestnuts,
   diced
2 cups Chinese cabbage (bok
   toi), diced
2 cups celery stalks, diced

1 cup Chinese pea pods, cut
   in two
1 teaspoon MSG
   (monosodium glutamate)
½ teaspoon sesame oil
½ teaspoon Chinese canned
   or bottled oyster sauce
1 teaspoon soy sauce
4 tablespoons cornstarch,
   dissolved in ¾ cup water
1 cup toasted almonds

Heat oil in skillet and add salt. Turn flame on full and add
chicken, searing until very light brown—about 2 minutes. Add
bamboo shoots, water chestnuts, greens, and celery. Stir well
and add the chicken broth. Cover skillet and cook for 3 minutes.
Remove cover and add pea pods. Stir and cook an additional 2
minutes. Add the MSG, sesame oil, oyster sauce and soy sauce.
Stir well and thicken with the dissolved cornstarch. Serve
topped with toasted almonds.

Drink suggestion: Rum drink

LAWRENCE OF OREGANO

ADDRESS   662 West Diversey Avenue
TELEPHONE   871-1916
HOURS AND DAYS   Mon.–Thurs. 11:30 A.M.–midnight; Fri., Sat.
     11:30 A.M.–1:00 A.M.; Sun. 3 P.M.–midnight
HOLIDAYS CLOSED   Thanksgiving, Christmas
RESERVATIONS   No
CREDIT CARDS   No
ENTERTAINMENT   Yes
PARKING   Reduced rate on Clark Street
BANQUET FACILITIES   No
DRESS   Casual
LIQUOR   Yes
WINE   Limited selection

Lettuce Entertain You Enterprises understands that waiting is usually not pleasant, so they have provided a large waiting area where the waiters and waitresses put on a musical show. The performers also stifle your hunger with complimentary garlic bread and eggplant. The restaurant is designed with an Italian deli in the front and the dining area in the back. You are welcome to sit in the bar area and enjoy the fun entertainment if you like. If you're dining, the baked mostaccioli, fettucine and veal marsala are all good choices.

Stuffed Artichoke

Serves 6

6 medium artichokes
  Juice of ½ lemon
½ pound white bread, crusts
  removed
1 pound butter, softened

1 tablespoon minced garlic
3 tablespoons chopped
  parsley
Salt and pepper

Trim the artichoke by cutting off the stem where it meets the body of the artichoke, so that it will stand up straight. Using kitchen shears or a small paring knife, remove the sharp pointy tips of each leaf. Immerse artichokes in boiling water, add the lemon juice and cook until you can easily pierce the stem with a fork. Remove from the boiling water and cool immediately in cold water. When cool, drain on paper towel and remove purple spiny material from inside of artichokes with a small teaspoon. Keep artichokes cold till ready to fill. *Stuffing:* Shred the bread into a bowl with the butter. Blend with the garlic and parsley. Adjust seasoning with a little salt and pepper. While mixture is still soft, stuff into the center of each artichoke, using all of the stuffing. Wrap each artichoke in aluminum foil and refrigerate before baking. To heat, place in a 375° oven for 15–20 minutes.

LAWRY'S THE PRIME RIB

ADDRESS   100 East Ontario Street
TELEPHONE   787-5000
HOURS AND DAYS   Lunch: Mon.–Fri. 11:30 A.M.–2 P.M.
          Dinner: Mon.–Thurs. 5–11 P.M.; Fri., Sat. 5 P.M.–
              midnight; Sun. 3–10 P.M.
HOLIDAYS CLOSED   Thanksgiving, Christmas
RESERVATIONS   Yes
CREDIT CARDS   AE, MC, VI
ENTERTAINMENT   No
PARKING   Valet
BANQUET FACILITIES   Up to 55
DRESS   Casual
LIQUOR   Yes
WINE   Good selection

The decor of Lawry's creates an exquisite setting, with a lovely lobby area for cocktails. The roast beef is excellent, and its high quality is consistent no matter what cut you prefer. In the bar area, hot appetizers or cheeses are served with your drinks from 4 to 7 P.M. Monday–Friday. Try their great special luncheon buffet, a good value. It includes a roast beef sandwich, salad bar, and coffee. The main dining room at lunch offers a fish of the day, chef's salad, an egg creation and, of course, their famous roast beef.

Eggs Maximilienne

Serves 2

2 large tomatoes
2 tablespoons chopped
   parsley
½ clove garlic, crushed
2 tablespoons grated
   Parmesan cheese

½ teaspoon butter
4 eggs
½ cup soft bread crumbs
   tossed with 2 tablespoons
   melted butter

Cut the tomatoes in half and scoop out the pulp. Sprinkle inside of tomato shells with a mixture of the parsley, garlic and cheese. Drop a bit of butter into each shell. Break an egg into each shell. Sprinkle crumbs generously over the eggs. Bake in a 375° oven for 10 minutes. Note: A fanciful dish—but not at all difficult to prepare.

Wine suggestion: Medium white Bordeaux, Alsatian or California wine

LEE'S CANTON CAFE

ADDRESS   2300 South Wentworth Avenue
TELEPHONE   225-4838
HOURS AND DAYS   Sun.–Thurs. 11 A.M.–midnight; Fri., Sat. 11
    A.M.–2 A.M.
HOLIDAYS CLOSED   None
RESERVATIONS   Not necessary
CREDIT CARDS   AE
ENTERTAINMENT   No
PARKING   Yes
BANQUET FACILITIES   Yes
DRESS   Casual
LIQUOR   No
WINE   Bring your own

    Lee's Canton Cafe, located in exciting Chinatown, specializes in genuine Cantonese dinners and Dem Sem (tea pastries). They have received many awards. Especially recommended is a first course of whole shrimp, steamed in the shell and served with a tangy sauce of soy and fresh onions. If you've got four or more in your party, try the fresh whole steamed pike, Chinese style—filleted at your table and served with flair!

Steamed Pike

Serves 4

Salt
1 pound fresh pike (12"–15"
long), scaled and cleaned
thoroughly
2 cups chicken stock
2 tablespoons chopped green
onion
½ cup shredded fresh ginger
½ teaspoon MSG
(monosodium glutamate)
4 tablespoons peanut oil

1 tablespoon white wine or
dry sherry
2 tablespoons soy sauce
2 tablespoons sugar
4 tablespoons Chinese
vinegar (rice-based)
2 tablespoons lotus root
starch or cornstarch,
mixed with 5 tablespoons
cold water
1 tablespoon sesame oil

Salt center cavity of fish and split lengthwise. Boil chicken stock
with green onion, ginger and MSG. Remove from heat. Put fish
in stock, return to heat and poach for 5 minutes, or until fish
flakes easily when tested with a fork. Put fish on platter; strain
from stock and place ginger and green onions on top of fish. *To
make sauce*, heat peanut oil, wine and 2 cups stock (used to
poach fish). Add soy sauce, sugar, vinegar and 2 teaspoons salt.
Boil. Then add lotus root starch or cornstarch paste. Cook until
thickened. Add sesame oil, stir gently and pour over fish.
Wine suggestion: Dry white Burgundy or California wine

THE LEFT BANK (RIVE GAUCHE)

ADDRESS   21145 Governor's Highway, Matteson
TELEPHONE   747-4545
HOURS AND DAYS   Tues.–Sun. 11:30 A.M.–2:30 P.M.; 5:30 P.M.–
        midnight
        Disco open daily
HOLIDAYS CLOSED   None
RESERVATIONS   Advised
CREDIT CARDS   All major cards
ENTERTAINMENT   Yes
PARKING   Doorman
BANQUET FACILITIES   Yes
DRESS   Jacket and tie for dinner
LIQUOR   Yes
WINE   Extensive selection

Start off your evening by dining in one of the four elegant rooms available at the Left Bank. The Burgundy Room seats you in Louis XV tapestry chairs. The Country Room creates a country French atmosphere. La Salle d'Argent has entertainment and a small dance floor. Le Carrousel is the discotheque designed with a circus theme. Horses from an old-fashioned merry-go-round line the dance floor. The French menu is the same in each room. An excellent first course to try is the Bisque Champignon, a fresh mushroom soup. The waiter, dressed in a tuxedo, prepares this at your table. We recommend the boneless breast of pheasant, capon or the roast of spring lamb. All entrees are served with outstanding fresh vegetables. After dinner, dance in the exciting disco, or visit the game room. An entire evening of superb dining and entertainment can be found at The Left Bank.

Bisque Champignon

Serves 4

3 cups chicken stock
1 pound mushroom stems
  and caps, finely chopped,
  plus 1 pound mushrooms,
  sliced

4 tablespoons butter
3 tablespoons flour
¼ teaspoon dry mustard
¼ cup cream sherry
½ cup heavy cream

Strain well-seasoned chicken stock. Add chopped mushroom stems and caps to stock, simmer 20–30 minutes and strain. In a sauce pan, melt butter and sauté sliced mushrooms lightly. Add flour and cook, stirring constantly, for 2 minutes. Add chicken stock and dry mustard. Cook, stirring constantly until liquid begins to thicken. Add cream sherry. Bring to boil, add heavy cream. Bring soup to a simmer (do not boil) and serve immediately.

Wine: Dry tawny Madeira

LOU MALNATI'S PIZZERIA

ADDRESS   6649 North Lincoln Avenue, Lincolnwood
TELEPHONE   673-0800
HOURS AND DAYS   Mon.–Fri. 11 A.M.–2 A.M.; Sat. noon–2 A.M.;
      Sun. 4 P.M.–1 A.M.
HOLIDAYS CLOSED   Thanksgiving, Christmas
RESERVATIONS   No
CREDIT CARDS   House card only
ENTERTAINMENT   No
PARKING   Ample
BANQUET FACILITIES   Up to 85
DRESS   Casual
LIQUOR   Yes
WINE   Limited house wines
OTHER LOCATIONS   3305 Vollmer Road, Flossmoor (698-6700),
      and 1050 Higgins, Elk Grove Village (439-2000).

In the mood for great pizza? Try this place for its famous thick-crusted pizza filled with lots of cheese and a variety of toppings. They are made in three different sizes, depending on your appetite. Salads are fresh and crisp and have a good flavor. You can eat well and very reasonably here. Also available are a few pastas and sandwiches. Service is very friendly.

Malnati Chicken

Serves 6–8

12 *pieces of chicken*
  Oil
½ *pound mushrooms, sliced*
 3 *tablespoons butter*
¼ *cup chopped parsley*

Juice of 1 lemon
4 *bouillon cubes*
3 *cups water*
½ *teaspoon powdered sage*

½ teaspoon powdered
rosemary
½ teaspoon powdered bay
leaf
Pinch of garlic powder

1 cup Marsala or sweet
sherry
1 cup white wine
1 medium onion, chopped
½ pint whipping cream
2 tablespoons flour

Lightly fry the chicken in oil until golden brown. Take out and drain on paper towels. Sauté mushrooms in 2 tablespoons of the butter; add parsley and lemon juice. Sauté 5 minutes and remove with slotted spoon from juice. To the juice, add bouillon cubes and water. Season with sage, rosemary, bay leaf and a bit of garlic powder to taste. Add ½ cup Marsala or sherry, and white wine. Bring to a boil. Add onion, let simmer for 3 minutes and remove from heat. Put chicken in a baking dish and cover with the mushrooms and parsley. Pour the broth over it and bake at 350° for 1 hour. Remove the chicken and put on a warm platter. Strain the juice and return to baking pan. Put mushrooms and onions strained from juice on the chicken. Put juice on hot fire and reduce it by half. With a spoon, skim fat. Add whipping cream, then add paste made from 1 tablespoon butter and the flour. Dissolve into sauce by stirring constantly. The sauce should look semi-thick and silky. Add remaining ½ cup Marsala or sherry. Remove from the fire. Add the chicken to sauce and mix. Put back in the oven for a few minutes and serve.

Wine suggestion: Dry white Italian wine

THE MAGIC PAN CREPERIE

ADDRESS 60 East Walton Street
TELEPHONE 943-2456
HOURS AND DAYS Mon.–Thurs. 11 A.M.–midnight; Fri., Sat. 11
A.M.–1 A.M.; Sun. 11 A.M.–9 P.M.
HOLIDAYS CLOSED All major holidays
RESERVATIONS Not necessary
CREDIT CARDS AE, MC, VI
ENTERTAINMENT No
PARKING No
BANQUET FACILITIES Yes
DRESS Casual
LIQUOR Yes
WINE Limited selection
OTHER LOCATIONS: Oakbrook Center, Oakbrook; Hawthorn
Center, Vernon Hills; Old Orchard, Skokie; Woodfield
Center, Schaumburg

The Magic Pan Creperie has the cheerful look of a European country inn with an abundance of live plants and lovely antiques. The name of the restaurant is taken from the patented wheel that rotates slowly over a ring of gas flames. After one revolution, the crepes are perfectly cooked and ready for any of the more than twenty different fillings for entree, dessert, Sunday brunch or après-theater. Our personal favorites are the sensational Spinach Soufflé crepe, sprinkled with Parmesan cheese and served with a cheese sauce; the Crab Delight, king crab in a light béchamel sauce with sherry; and the Crepes Ratatouille, fresh vegetables simmered together and folded in a crepe. Their fresh avocado or spinach salad is a tasty addition for lunch or dinner.

Basic Crepe

12–14 crepes

1 cup flour
  Pinch of salt
3 eggs

1½ cups milk
  ½ cup oil

Sift the flour and salt together into a mixing bowl. Add eggs and mix together. Add milk gradually and beat until mixture is smooth. The batter should have the consistency of heavy cream. Let stand for 2 hours before using.

Brush a hot crepe pan with oil. Pour in 1½–2 tablespoons of batter. Tip the pan to coat it with a thin layer of batter. When the crepe is golden brown (in about 1 minute) turn it and brown the other side. Continue cooking crepes, adding oil to pan when needed.

STRAWBERRY CREPES SUPREME

Serves 6

6 cups strawberries, sliced
  (reserve 6 perfect berries for
  garnish)
1¼ cups brown sugar

6 cooked crepes
1 cup sour cream
  Powdered sugar

Toss the strawberries gently with ¾ cup brown sugar. Place 1 cup of sweetened strawberries in center of each crepe. Top each serving with 2 tablespoons of sour cream. Sprinkle 1 tablespoon brown sugar over sour cream. Fold sides of crepe over center to enclose filling. Sprinkle powdered sugar over filled crepe. Top each crepe with 2 teaspoons of sour cream. Sprinkle brown sugar over each serving and top with a whole strawberry.
Wine suggestion: Sweet white Bordeaux

LA MARGARITA

ADDRESS   868 North Wabash Avenue, Chicago, or 6319 West
           Dempster Street, Morton Grove
TELEPHONE   Chicago (751-3434), Morton Grove (966-5037)
HOURS AND DAYS   Sun.–Fri. 11 A.M.–4 A.M.; Sat. 11 A.M.–5 A.M.
HOLIDAYS CLOSED   Christmas
RESERVATIONS   Suggested
CREDIT CARDS   All major cards
ENTERTAINMENT   Strolling guitarist
PARKING   Morton Grove only
BANQUET FACILITIES   Morton Grove only
DRESS   Casual
LIQUOR   Yes
WINE   Limited selection

      Tortilla chips with a very spicy relish dip are complimentary as you sit down to an experience in Mexican cooking at La Margarita. Tacos, tamales, enchiladas, skirt steaks and combination plates are all available. Strolling guitarists provide gaiety while dining. Service is pleasant and accommodating. For a memorable evening start by trying our personal suggestion: order the Guacamole and put it on top of an order of Quesaillas. Try different dishes like Tostadas (open-face tacos, with your choice of beef, chicken or sausage, topped with slices of avocado), Chilaquiles (tortilla strips with bits of chicken in tomato sauce, topped with melted cheese and sour cream) and Paella (shrimp, lobster, chicken, clams, and vegetables served on rice).

Tacos

Serves 6

1 chopped onion
½ green pepper
Corn oil
1 pound ground beef (or chicken)
1 8-ounce can tomato sauce
1 teaspoon chili powder

Salt and pepper to taste
1 head lettuce, shredded
Small bowl sharp grated cheese
12 tortillas
2 solid tomatoes, diced

Sauté the chopped onion and green pepper in 1 tablespoon corn oil until they are limp. Then add meat, mix and crumble. Brown for five minutes and pour in tomato sauce, chili powder, salt and pepper. Simmer over a low heat for half an hour, until the meat is crumbly and fairly dry. Just before you are ready to serve, prepare bowls of shredded lettuce and grated cheese. Then fold the tortillas, add the meat filling, hold with tongs and fry quickly in hot oil. The tacos should be golden and slightly firm, but not hard. Add tomato, then lettuce; and then sprinkle cheese over the entire serving.

Drink suggestion: Mexican beer

MAXIM'S DE PARIS

ADDRESS   1300 North Astor Street
TELEPHONE   943-1111; reservations 943-1136
HOURS AND DAYS   Lunch: Mon.–Sat. noon–3 P.M.
         Dinner: Mon.–Thurs. and Sun. 6 P.M.–midnight; Fri.,
         Sat. 6 P.M.–1 A.M.
HOLIDAYS CLOSED   All major holidays
RESERVATIONS   Yes
CREDIT CARDS   All major cards
ENTERTAINMENT   Music and dancing
PARKING   Available
BANQUET FACILITIES   Yes
DRESS   Jacket and tie
LIQUOR   Yes
WINE   Extensive selection

Maxim's de Paris is a replica of the famous restaurant of the same name in Paris. It creates the same romantic atmosphere with soothing music and art nouveau decor. The authentic French cuisine offers excellent specialities such as Sole Albert (Dover sole cooked in French vermouth), Veal Orloff (medallion of veal with a purée of mushrooms, served with a mornay sauce) and the Coquilles St. Jacques (bay scallops cooked in white wine and shallots). The Crepe Veuve Joyeuse, a French pancake stuffed with lemon soufflé, is an unbelievably great dessert and worth its price of $3.75 per person. The interesting and superb menu offered is completely a la carte.

Coquilles St. Jacques aux Petits Legumes

Serves 4–6

2 medium carrots
1 celery root
1 cucumber
1½ pounds bay scallops
1 teaspoon finely chopped
   shallots

2 large tomatoes, peeled and
   chopped
1 cup white wine
3 ounces (6 tablespoons)
   butter
Chopped parsley

Cut carrots, celery root and cucumber into attractive small pieces with a melon ball spoon or teaspoon. Then cook in water until almost done but not too soft. Put the scallops, shallots, carrots, celery root, cucumber, tomatoes and wine into a pan and bring to a boil. Reduce heat and simmer for 5 minutes. Remove everything from the pan except the juices, which are to be reduced by half. After reducing the juices, add the butter in small pieces. Add the scallops and all the vegetables. Bring almost to a boil and sprinkle with chopped parsley just before serving.

Wine suggestion: Dry white Burgundy or California wine

MEL MARKON'S

ADDRESS   2150 North Lincoln Park West
TELEPHONE   525-5550
HOURS AND DAYS   Mon.–Fri. 11–4 A.M.; Sat. 9 A.M.–5 A.M.;
        Sun. 9 A.M.–4 A.M.
HOLIDAYS CLOSED   Christmas
RESERVATIONS   No
CREDIT CARDS   No
ENTERTAINMENT   No
PARKING   Doorman
BANQUET FACILITIES   None, but large groups can be
        accommodated
DRESS   Casual
LIQUOR   Yes
WINE   Limited house wines

   A unique casual atmosphere exists here with hanging ferns and displays of modern arts and crafts by local Chicago artists. The food and drinks are also unique, fun and good. The speciality items include cabbage borscht, onion soup, a Reuben sandwich, avocado and Monterey Jack cheese with fresh bean sprouts, Steak Teriyaki and Chicken Oriental. The fresh strawberry cheesecake is an absolute must! Many cleverly named drinks are available which are various combinations of refreshing fruit juices and liquor. A fabulous late-night menu is available with many interesting and tasty selections.

Hot Sweet and Sour Cabbage Soup with Short Ribs

Serves 4–6

3–4 *short ribs*
  1 *teaspoon garlic powder*
  1 *onion, sliced thin*
  2 *cups mashed tomatoes*
  2 *cups tomato catsup*

1 *cup white sugar*
4 *teaspoons lemon juice*
⅛ *teaspoon salt*
1 *small cabbage, chopped in*
  ½" *square pieces*

Put ribs, garlic powder and onion in a pot and fill with hot water; cook approximately one hour or until ribs are tender. When ribs are done, remove, cut into small pieces and put back into pot with all remaining ingredients. Keep at a boil for approximately 20–30 minutes or until cabbage is cooked.

Wine suggestion: Red Burgundy-type wine

MEL MARKON'S ZANADU

ADDRESS   6259 North Broadway Avenue
TELEPHONE   338-3700
HOURS AND DAYS   Mon.–Fri. 5 P.M.–1:30 A.M.; Sat. 5 P.M.–2:30
      A.M.; Sun. 4 P.M.–1:30 A.M.
HOLIDAYS CLOSED   Christmas
RESERVATIONS   No
CREDIT CARDS   No
ENTERTAINMENT   Music in restaurant and upper deck level;
      disco separate from dining area
PARKING   Private parking lot ½ block from restaurant on west
      side of street
BANQUET FACILITIES   No
DRESS   Casual
LIQUOR   Yes
WINE   Limited house wines

Mel Markon's Zanadu is truly a "Pleasure Palace," an atmosphere inspired by the opening lines of the Coleridge poem "Kubla Khan": "In Xanadu did Kubla Khan / A stately pleasure-dome decree." Karen and Tony Barone, famed restaurant designers, have created a most unusual and exciting restaurant with 29-foot ceilings constructed of countless arching domes, and an illuminated space capsule carrying drinks between the multiple levels for eating, drinking and dancing. The "pleasure-dome" theme is carried out with the foods offered, such as banana french toast, french-fried ice cream and the famous Zanabana drink. The favorites that we've enjoyed are the spinach chopped steak, (a chopped steak with fresh spinach, melted Swiss cheese and Parmesan cheese), and the seafood crepes. There's a good selection of scrumptious soups, including mushroom barley and hot sweet and sour cabbage borscht.

Mornay Sauce

6 cups

9 *tablespoons butter*
1 *ounce (2 tablespoons)*
   whole pine nuts
9 *tablespoons flour*
½ *teaspoon salt*

¾ *cup Harveys Bristol*
   Cream Sherry
1 *teaspoon chopped chives*
5 *ounces Gruyère cheese,*
   grated
4 *cups half and half*

In a large saucepan, melt butter. Sauté pine nuts for a minute or two. Add flour and cook, stirring, until butter and flour are well mixed. Add salt, sherry, chives and cheese and mix all together with wire whisk. Then add warm half and half slowly, using the whisk constantly, until thickened. This sauce may be used over fish, seafood, poultry or green vegetables.

MESON DEL LAGO

ADDRESS   158 East Ontario Street
TELEPHONE   649-9215
HOURS AND DAYS   Lunch: Mon.–Sat. 11:30 A.M.–3 P.M.
    Dinner: Mon.–Sat. 5–11:30 P.M.
HOLIDAYS CLOSED   Memorial Day, Labor Day, Thanksgiving,
    New Year's Day
RESERVATIONS   Yes
CREDIT CARDS   All major cards
ENTERTAINMENT   Yes, including at lunch time
PARKING   Doorman
BANQUET FACILITIES   Up to 250
DRESS   Informal
LIQUOR   Yes
WINE   Limited selection

In the mood for a night in Mexico? Enter this lovely restaurant with strolling guitarists playing the cheery authentic songs and music, walls covered with Mexican tiles, a flowing fountain and two skylights with fresh plants hanging from the ceiling. Enjoy the taco bar where you can make your own taco with the usual ingredients, such as guacamole, chopped onion, cheeses, tomatoes, refried beans, chicken, ground beef and other specials of the day. It's offered at Saturday brunch and dinner—available only at dinner time on other days. For a little taste of a variety of foods try the "Combination Memo," or order the Enchiladas Con Mole (chicken with a mole sauce) or one of the omelets; and for dessert try the Black Bottom Pie.

Guacamole

Serves 6–8

3 medium avocados
1 small white onion
1 medium tomato

½ cup cilantro (available at Mexican, Japanese or Chinese markets)
Salt and pepper

Cut avocados in half and remove the seeds. Peel flesh and mash roughly (leave chunks in it). Dice onion, tomato, and cilantro. Add to avocado. Season with salt and pepper to taste. Put avocado seed in dip so it won't turn black. Serve with warm tortillas and top with sour cream.

Drink suggestion: Dos Equis (Mexican beer)

MI CASA-SU CASA

ADDRESS   2524 North Southport Avenue
TELEPHONE   525-6323
HOURS AND DAYS   Mon.–Fri. 11:30 A.M.–11:30 P.M.; Sat. 4 P.M.–
      2 A.M.; Sun. 4 P.M.–midnight
HOLIDAYS CLOSED   Thanksgiving, Christmas
RESERVATIONS   Suggested
CREDIT CARDS   All major cards
ENTERTAINMENT   Strolling guitars
PARKING   No
BANQUET FACILITIES   Up to 80
DRESS   Casual
LIQUOR   Yes
WINE   Limited selection

Mi Casa is an extremely good Mexican restaurant where it is possible to get a nice variety of authentic Mexican dishes. To start off the meal, the Camuch (tortilla chips, tomato sauce and beans, topped with lots of cheese) is a real treat. Skirt steaks, chicken with rice, enchiladas and sopes (tortillas covered with beans, avocado and cheese) are outstanding. Service is cordial, and you can enjoy your meal at a leisurely pace. It is a cozy, comfortable place. Why not have a piña colada or dark Mexican beer to start your meal?

Enchiladas Suizas

Serves 6

1 2- to 2½-pound spring
  chicken
Water
Salt
1 onion, sliced

16 tortillas
½ cup oil
  Sauce (see below)
½ pound longhorn cheese,
  grated

Cook chicken in water with salt and onion; when done, remove the bones and break meat into small pieces. Lightly fry each tortilla in ½ cup oil for a few seconds. Add a little sauce to chicken to moisten and add color. Put 1 tablespoon of chicken into each fried tortilla. Roll up and put in ovenproof casserole. Add 3 spoonfuls of sauce over each enchilada. Cover with cheese and place in preheated oven at 300° until the cheese is completely melted. Serve immediately.

SAUCE

1 large onion, diced
1 6-ounce can tomato paste
  Black pepper

¼ cup oil
1 clove garlic
1 8-ounce can tomatoes

Sauté onion, tomato paste and black pepper in ¼ cup oil. Blend garlic and tomatoes in blender until smooth. Add the garlic mixture to the sauce and simmer for half an hour.

Drink suggestion: Mexican beer

THE MILK PAIL

ADDRESS   R.R. 2, Dundee (on Highway 25, between Elgin and
        Dundee)
TELEPHONE   742-5040
HOURS AND DAYS   Tues.–Fri. 11 A.M.–9 P.M.; Sat. 11 A.M.–10
        P.M.; Sun. 9 A.M.–9 P.M.
HOLIDAYS CLOSED   Christmas, New Year's Day
RESERVATIONS   Accepted Tues.–Sat., not on Sun.
CREDIT CARDS   AE
ENTERTAINMENT   Piano on Fri. and Sat. evenings (Cocktail
        Lounge)
PARKING   Yes
BANQUET FACILITIES   Only during winter months
DRESS   Casual
LIQUOR   Yes
WINE   Limited house wines

This family-type restaurant is located in a country setting. There is a wide variety of selections on the menu—from a
sandwich and a salad to pheasant and strip steak. The food is
not only homemade but home grown. Recommended specialties
are the duck, pheasant, fried chicken, rainbow trout and, fresh
from the oven, pastries that make your mouth water. A real
treat is the delicious Sunday brunch. You'll appreciate the generous portions. Six adjoining specialty shops feature their own
baked goods, gifts, children's wear and art.

Roast Pheasant with Wild Rice Dressing

Serves 2-3

1 *pheasant*
Salt, pepper, MSG,
poultry seasoning

Dressing (see below)
Brandy Sauce (see below)

Preheat oven to 400°. Season pheasant cavities lightly with salt, pepper and MSG, then stuff with the dressing. Tie legs to tail to keep dressing in bird. Fold wings under back to keep shape of bird while roasting. Place in pan and season outside of bird thoroughly with salt, pepper, poultry seasoning and MSG. Cover bottom of pan with a small amount of water and place in oven. Roast for 1½–2 hours, depending on age of bird. To test for doneness, pierce thick part of breast and press underneath. If liquid comes out pink, bird is not yet done. If you have more dressing than needed for pheasant, place in covered casserole and bake for the last 30 minutes of roasting time. Serve with Brandy Sauce.

Wine suggestion: Dry red Bordeaux

DRESSING

½ *cup chopped celery*
½ *cup chopped onion*
2 *tablespoons butter*
8 *cups chopped bread*
2 *cups cooked long grain*
  wild rice
¼ *teaspoon salt*
  Pinch white pepper

1 *tablespoon sage*
1 *tablespoon celery seed*
1 *tablespoon MSG*
  (monosodium glutamate)
1 *teaspoon poultry*
  seasoning
  Poultry stock (enough to
  moisten bread)

Sauté the celery and onion in butter until brown. Then mix all ingredients thoroughly in a large bowl.

BRANDY SAUCE

Drippings
½ cup chopped onion
2 tablespoons butter
½ cup flour

½ cup brandy
2 cups peach juice
Seasonings

Remove all oil from drippings in roasting pan. Chop ½ cup onion and sauté in 2 tablespoons butter until brown. Add ½ cup flour slowly. Mix well to a creamy roux. Add ½ cup of good brandy, 2 cups peach juice, and degreased drippings. Season with a pinch each of sugar, salt, pepper and MSG. Bring to boil and serve.

MYRON AND PHIL'S STEAK AND LOBSTER HOUSE

ADDRESS 3900 West Devon Avenue, Lincolnwood
    111 Skokie Boulevard, Northbrook
TELEPHONE 677-6663 (Lincolnwood), 835-3600 (Northbrook)
HOURS AND DAYS Lincolnwood: Mon.–Fri. 11:30 A.M.–12:30
    A.M., Sat. 5 P.M.–2 A.M.; Sun. 4 P.M.–midnight
    Northbrook: Mon.–Fri. 7 A.M.–12:30 A.M.; Sat. 7 A.M.–2
    A.M.; Sun. 9 A.M.–midnight
HOLIDAYS CLOSED Thanksgiving, Christmas, Jewish High Holy
    Days
RESERVATIONS Until 6:30 P.M.
CREDIT CARDS All major cards
ENTERTAINMENT Tues.–Sat.
PARKING Attendant
BANQUET FACILITIES No
DRESS Informal
LIQUOR Yes
WINE Limited selection

These family-run restaurants have a strong interest in maintaining high standards and they do so successfully. They are attractive, cozy and comfortable. Service is very friendly and quite efficient. There is nicely done pepper steak, butt steak, fresh trout and red snapper. The relish tray comes with the dinner, and everything on it is tasty. If you are looking for a spot to have a late night snack, there is a wide variety of foods at lower prices after 10 P.M. The omelet, crabmeat in avocado and chocolate sundaes are all good.

Pepper Steak

Serves 4

2½ pounds boneless filet
    mignon, cut into squares
    Garlic salt, pepper, MSG
5 tablespoons butter
½ pound mushrooms, sliced

1 green pepper, sliced
1 onion, sliced
4 fresh tomatoes, quartered
½ jigger Burgundy
    Sauce (see below)

Dip meat in mixture of garlic, salt, pepper and MSG. Brown meat in 2 tablespoons butter. Cook until tender, about 15 minutes. Sauté mushrooms, green pepper and onion in remaining butter for 5 minutes, add tomatoes and cook for 2 minutes more. Just before serving, add Burgundy. Pour sauce over the meat and vegetables and serve at once.

SAUCE

3 cups water
3 beef bones (also add meat
    that may be around for
    more flavor)
1 large onion
3 tomatoes
3 green peppers

1 tablespoon MSG
    (monosodium glutamate)
1 cup Worcestershire sauce
2 tablespoons whole
    peppercorns
1 pound butter
1½ cups flour

Cook all ingredients except peppercorns, butter and flour very slowly for 3 hours; strain. Wrap peppercorns in cheesecloth and pound to break into bits. Add pepper, butter, and flour to sauce and stir until it thickens.

Wine suggestion: Medium red California wine

NIELSEN'S

ADDRESS   7330 West North Avenue, Elmwood Park
TELEPHONE   453-9200; Chicago number 625-8000
HOURS AND DAYS   Mon.–Sat. 11:30 A.M.–11:30 P.M.; Sun.
     noon–9 P.M.
HOLIDAYS CLOSED   Christmas Eve and the first Monday in July
RESERVATIONS   Accepted
CREDIT CARDS   CB, MC, VI, house card
ENTERTAINMENT   No
PARKING   Ample
BANQUET FACILITIES   Up to 400
DRESS   Casual
LIQUOR   Yes
WINE   Limited selection

     The owner of Nielsen's, Erik Jensen, has transformed a smorgasbord restaurant into an intimate family restaurant. This is a sure family favorite with great service and excellent food. The large and imaginative menu offers such exciting and delightful dishes as the Salmon Anna Marie (cooked in whiskey with onions and mushrooms), Danish Red Spot (flounder) and Filet Mignon a la Gordola. The meatball appetizers are very tasty and come with the dinner. Nielsen's was honored by the presence of Her Royal Highness Queen Margrethe II and Prince Henrik of Denmark at a luncheon in her honor.

Danish Holiday Soup

Serves 12 or more

BROTH

1 *medium stewing hen*   1 *parsley root*
4 *beef knuckles*   1 *small celery root*
3 *large carrots*   Salt
3–4 *leeks*

Place the hen and beef knuckles in a large pan. Cover with cold water, bring to boil and carefully skim. Then add carrots, the tops of leeks (onions may be substituted), the parsley root and the celery root (or half a stalk of celery). As simmering continues, keep skimming to keep broth absolutely clear. Add salt to taste. When hen is tender, remove. It can be used for additional garnish or reserved for other use, such as salad or sandwiches. The soup should cook 6–8 hours and then be strained; reserve and dice the vegetables for garnish.

MEATBALLS

1 *pound finely ground meat*   *Salt and pepper to taste*
   (*veal, beef, pork*)   1–2 *tablespoons grated onion*
3 *tablespoons flour*   ½ *cup milk, lukewarm*
2 *eggs*

Mix together ground meat, flour, eggs, salt, pepper and onion. Mix well and add milk. Shape into small balls and drop into boiling, lightly salted water, or some of the broth. Cook until meat is done to taste.

DUMPLINGS

½ cup (1 stick) butter   2–3 eggs
1 cup boiling water   Pinch of salt and pepper
1 cup flour

Add butter to boiling water; when melted, add flour all at once. Stir well over the fire, remove from heat and continue to stir until slightly cooled. Add eggs and a little salt and pepper; mix thoroughly. Form with spoon into small dumplings and boil as for meatballs, approximately 3 minutes.

To serve, add the meatballs and dumplings to strained broth, together with finely diced carrots, celery, parsley root and leeks. *Drink suggestion: Aquavit, followed by Danish light beer*

THE NINETY-FIFTH

ADDRESS   172 East Chestnut Street (John Hancock Center)
TELEPHONE   787-9596
HOURS AND DAYS   Lunch: Mon.–Sat. noon–3 P.M.
         Dinner: Mon.–Sat. 6 P.M.–midnight; Sun. 6–10 P.M.
HOLIDAYS CLOSED   Memorial Day, Christmas, New Year's Day
RESERVATIONS   Yes
CREDIT CARDS   All major cards
ENTERTAINMENT   Combo for dancing in Sybaris Lounge on
         96th floor
PARKING   Self-park in John Hancock Building garage
BANQUET FACILITIES   Yes
DRESS   Semi-casual
LIQUOR   Yes
WINE   Extensive selection

Located on the 95th floor of the John Hancock Center, The Ninety-Fifth offers a spectacular view of four states. The decor is bold and modern, and the menu is French. This elegant restaurant has won many awards, including the Ivy Award given by *Institution* magazine as the most professional restaurant of 1975. It has also been a *Holiday* Award winner for the past five years. The Beef Wellington is our personal favorite. The Scallopini of Veal Cote D'Azur (veal sautéed in a cream sauce and lightly seasoned with Pernod, Madeira and mushrooms) is also delightful. Their fantastic pastry chef creates tempting choices for dessert. The extensive menu is all a la carte.

Turbot Poche Florentine

Serves 2

1 stick plus 3 tablespoons
   unsalted butter
2 tablespoons chopped
   shallots
1 cup sliced mushrooms
2 6-ounce pieces of turbot
   (cleaned and skinned)
½ cup plus 2 tablespoons
   Chablis

Salt and pepper to taste
1 cup chopped, cooked
   spinach
4 egg yolks
   Juice of 1 lemon
⅓ cup heavy cream
1 tablespoon flour

Preheat oven to 350°. Melt 1 tablespoon butter in a hot oven-proof skillet and sauté the shallots and mushrooms. Add the turbot, ½ cup wine, salt and pepper and bring to boil. Place skillet in oven for 20 minutes. While turbot is cooking, heat spinach in small saucepan with 1 tablespoon butter, season and keep hot in an ovenproof serving dish. Now prepare the hollandaise sauce. In the top of a double boiler, beat 4 egg yolks vigorously with lemon juice and 2 tablespoons wine until mixture is light and fluffy. Heat the 1 stick of butter until melted; add slowly to sauce and continue to beat until it reaches a smooth and creamy consistency. Set aside. Remove turbot from oven and place the fish in a pan with the spinach. To the mushroom sauce remaining in the skillet add the cream and cook for 5 minutes, stirring constantly. Make a paste by mixing 1 table-spoon butter with the flour and add to sauce to thicken. Combine with the hollandaise sauce. Pour the sauce over turbot. Place turbot under broiler until golden color.
Wine suggestion: Medium white Bordeaux

THE NITE-N-GALE

ADDRESS   346 Waukegan Avenue, Highwood
TELEPHONE   432-9744
HOURS AND DAYS   Lunch: Daily 11 A.M.–2 P.M.
          Dinner: Sun.–Thurs. 4 P.M.–midnight; Fri., Sat. 11
          A.M.–1 A.M.
HOLIDAYS CLOSED   Thanksgiving, Christmas
RESERVATIONS   Before 6 P.M.
CREDIT CARDS   House card
ENTERTAINMENT   Progressive jazz on Sat. nights in bar
PARKING   Yes
BANQUET FACILITIES   Small parties
DRESS   Casual
LIQUOR   Yes
WINE   Limited selection

There's a choice of two atmospheres at the Nite-N-Gale: a family restaurant or a cozy bar that provides entertainment on Saturday nights. Specials during the week are less expensive the night they are offered: Whitefish on Tues.; Prime Rib on Wed.; King Crab Legs on Thurs.; Lobster Tail on Fri. They're also known for their excellent ribs, french-fried shrimp, and deep-dish pizza. All the food is tasty and well prepared, and the service is friendly and efficient.

French-Fried Mushrooms

Serves 8

3 eggs	Garlic salt, salt, pepper to
2 cups milk	taste
2 cups bread crumbs	2 tablespoons sugar
1 cup flour	2 pounds mushrooms
	Oil for deep frying

Beat the eggs and milk together. Mix the bread crumbs and flour with garlic salt, salt, pepper and sugar. Wash the mushrooms and dip them into the egg mixture and then into the dry ingredients, then into eggs and dry ingredients again. Let stand for 15 minutes so coating will stick. Deep fry in hot oil (325°-350°) until brown.

LES OEUFS

ADDRESS   163 East Walton Place (Playboy Towers)
TELEPHONE   337-7330
HOURS AND DAYS   Tues.–Sat. 10 A.M.–midnight; Sun. 10 A.M.–
       11 P.M.
HOLIDAYS CLOSED   All major holidays
RESERVATIONS   No
CREDIT CARDS   MC, AE, CB, DC, VI, Playboy
ENTERTAINMENT   No
PARKING   No
BANQUET FACILITIES   No
DRESS   Casual
LIQUOR   Yes
WINE   Limited selection

This attractive setting is filled with antiques. Most objects in the restaurant are for sale. A full salad bar and soup bar are available. Everyday specials include fish, meat and chicken. Most dishes are a successful variety of ingredients mixed with eggs. Of particular note are the Omelet Lorraine (bacon, Monterey Jack and Parmesan cheeses inside), The Carlsbad (eggs, mushrooms and chives), Omelet Divan (filled with chicken and broccoli, served with Mornay sauce), and Omelet Kodiak (sweet morsels of crabmeat). Cheerful and friendly service is found here.

Omelet Kodiak

Serves 1

3 ounces crabmeat
4 tablespoons butter or
  margarine
3 fresh eggs

¼ teaspoon salt
⅛ teaspoon pepper
1 teaspoon chopped chives

Sauté crabmeat in 1 tablespoon of the butter, then keep it warm. Beat eggs with a fork; add salt and pepper. Heat pan, swirl the rest of the butter around in it with a fork and add eggs immediately. Stir eggs clockwise with fork, and let cook. When eggs are moist on top and set on bottom, place crabmeat filling on upper half, near handle. Roll omelet with a fork. Complete rolling and hold over a warm plate, turn omelet out into it. Garnish with chives.

Wine suggestion: Medium white California wine

OSCAR'S

ADDRESS   9040 Waukegan Road, Morton Grove
TELEPHONE   965-1977
HOURS AND DAYS   Mon.–Thurs. 11:30 A.M.–10 P.M.; Fri., Sat.
        11:30 A.M.–11 P.M.; Sun. noon–10 P.M.
HOLIDAYS CLOSED   Thanksgiving, Christmas
RESERVATIONS   No
CREDIT CARDS   All major cards
ENTERTAINMENT   No
PARKING   Yes
BANQUET FACILITIES   No
DRESS   Casual to formal
LIQUOR   Yes
WINE   Limited selection

Oscar's was established as a family business in 1930. Still owned and operated by the Fausts, Oscar's has maintained its reputation for excellent seafood and choice steaks. There are specials offered on both the luncheon and dinner menus. All the food is well prepared with good quality and flavor, especially the red snapper, whitefish and Shrimp de Jonghe. Beef is equally well represented.

Braised Short Ribs of Beef

Serves 3

*Short ribs (1 pound per
person)
Black pepper
2 cups water (or stock)*

*2 cloves garlic, chopped
½ cup roughly chopped
onion
½ cup tomato purée*

Sprinkle short ribs moderately with black pepper. Cook in baking pan at 375° for half an hour, then add water, garlic and onions. Lower heat to 325° and cook another half hour. Add tomato purée and cook for one hour more, turning meat in juice and adding water, if necessary, to prevent drying. Remove ribs, place in clean baking pan, cover with foil, and cook until tender (about 45 minutes). NOTE: Stock can be used in place of water, and remaining juices can be used as base for gravy.

Wine suggestion: Medium red Chianti

LE PERROQUET

ADDRESS   70 East Walton Place
TELEPHONE   944-7990
HOURS AND DAYS   Lunch: Mon.–Fri. noon–3 P.M.
        Dinner: Mon.–Sat. 6–10 P.M.
HOLIDAYS CLOSED   All major holidays
RESERVATIONS   Preferred
CREDIT CARDS   AE, DC
ENTERTAINMENT   No
PARKING   Available at garage next door
BANQUET FACILITIES   No
DRESS   Jacket and tie
LIQUOR   Yes
WINE   Extensive selection

A European-styled private elevator takes you to the third floor, for a truly unforgettable experience in dining. The decor is contemporary, airy and understated. Each table is elegantly set with the finest linens, china and fresh flowers. The highly impressive service tends to make one feel like royalty. The food is always fresh and delectable. The total feeling at Le Perroquet definitely rates an A+. They were given five stars by the Mobil Guide and awards from *Holiday* magazine and *Mainliner* (United Airlines). It's difficult to give recommendations, as every item offered deserves merit. Their pâtés are consistently outstanding. Pay close attention to the specialties of the day as they are usually a good choice; they are chosen according to the freshest items available in the market that day. Jovan Trboyevic, the owner, offers the most fabulous dessert soufflés that can be found. The dinners are priced at $19.50 per person.

Squabs with Sausage and Sauerkraut

Serves 6

2½ tablespoons butter
¼ pound sliced smoked ham
2 pounds sauerkraut
3 squabs
1 bouquet garni (1 bay leaf,
  1 sprig parsley, pinch of
  thyme, 1 stalk celery)
2–3 carrots

2–3 onions
6 debretzin sausages (may
  substitute any spicy
  sausage)
2 cups chicken consommé
1 cup dry white wine
  (about)

Rub the bottom of a large casserole with the butter and line it with half the ham. Drain the sauerkraut well and arrange it on top of the ham. Clean and split the squabs in half and place on top of the sauerkraut. Add the bouquet garni. Peel and slice the carrots and onions and spread them over the top. Add sausages and remaining ham. Pour in consommé and enough white wine to half submerge mixture. Cover casserole tightly and simmer on low heat for 1¾–2 hours. When squabs are tender, drain casserole of liquid and discard bouquet garni. Arrange the sauerkraut in the center of a large heated platter and surround it with the ham and sausage. Put the squab on top and serve with boiled potatoes.

Wine suggestion: Dry white Alsatian wine

PIZZERIA DUE

ADDRESS   619 North Wabash Avenue
TELEPHONE   943-2400
HOURS AND DAYS   Mon.–Fri. 11:30 A.M.–3:20 A.M.; Sat. 5 P.M.–
    4:20 A.M.; Sun. 4 P.M.–12:20 A.M.
HOLIDAYS CLOSED   Christmas, New Year's Day
RESERVATIONS   Yes
CREDIT CARDS   No
ENTERTAINMENT   No
PARKING   No
BANQUET FACILITIES   Yes
DRESS   Casual
LIQUOR   Yes
WINE   Limited house wines
OTHER LOCATION: Pizzeria Uno, 29 East Ohio (321-1000)

Bacchus, the God of Wine, welcomes you as you enter
Pizzeria Due. This bust was a tribute to the wines of the Pied-
mont Provinces in the eighteenth century. Inside, you will experience crisp, thick pizza made with cheeses imported from Italy.
Their small-sized pizza and tasty Italian salad is definitely
enough for two hungry adults. The menu is repeated at Pizzeria
Uno. For those in your group not in a pizza mood, the Poorboy
sandwich, a combination of sausage, salami and cheese, is good
and filling. You'll pay an average of $3.00–$3.50 per person for a
tasty meal.

Special Salad

Serves 4

1 cup cauliflower, broken
  into flowerets
1 cup grated carrots
½ cup onions, diced
½ cup celery, diced
½ cup black olives, sliced
¼ cup sweet peppers, diced
2 teaspoons sugar
⅔ cup wine vinegar

Crisp greens
2 tomatoes, cut up
1 Spanish onion, cut in
  rings
Salami, as desired
Swiss cheese, as desired
Wine vinegar-and-oil
  dressing
Parmesan cheese, grated

Marinate cauliflower, carrots, onions, celery, olives and sweet peppers in sugar and vinegar for 3 hours. Combine remaining ingredients except cheese and toss lightly. Top with the grated cheese.

PLENTYWOOD FARM

ADDRESS   130 South Church Road, Bensenville
TELEPHONE   766-0250; Chicago number 625-5220
HOURS AND DAYS   Lunch: Tues.–Sat. 11:30 A.M.–2:30 P.M.
    Dinner: Tues.–Sat. 5–9 P.M. (traditional); 6–10:30 P.M.
    (gourmet); Sun. noon–7 P.M.
HOLIDAYS CLOSED   Christmas Eve, Christmas
RESERVATIONS   Yes
CREDIT CARDS   AE, MC
ENTERTAINMENT   Piano
PARKING   Yes
BANQUET FACILITIES   Yes
DRESS   Casual
LIQUOR   Yes
WINE   Good selection

This family-run restaurant, just minutes by car from O'Hare airport, is a little world of charm and delight. The excellence of the food is combined with the warmth of its atmosphere and service. You'll love Plentywood's unusual yet reasonable menu, featuring really good Continental and traditional American cuisine. Plentywood Farm, a Chicago tradition, has won many awards since founder Katharine Howell first opened in 1932. At night, there are four different rooms with the same traditional, moderately priced menu. We recommend the French Lamb Chops, Steak Tartare, Steak Diane, Dover Sole, Veal Cordon Bleu and the Scampi Provençale (large shrimp with tomatoes and mushrooms). End your fine dining with Bombe Alaska or Chocolate Mousse, or try the Peach Melba.

Veal en Papillote

Serves 6

6 pieces parchment paper,
  24" × 16" each
Oil
12 large mushroom caps
6 large artichoke hearts, cut
  in half

12 4-ounce slices of veal, each
  ¼" thick
1 quart bordelaise sauce,
  cooled

Cut each sheet of parchment paper in the shape of a large heart, then brush with oil. Fold paper in half, make a small fold in open side, then start folding from point, overlapping to form an airtight seal. Make folds about halfway up heart, leaving opening, which will be sealed later. Place a mushroom cap and an artichoke half on each of 6 veal slices; cover with the remaining 6 slices. Insert one "sandwich" into opening of each parchment package. Add 3–4 ounces (6–8 tablespoons) of bordelaise sauce to cover the pieces of veal. Finish overlapping and folding the paper so that it becomes airtight and no steam can escape. Bake in 350° oven for about 20 minutes. Do not burn the bag. Heat remaining sauce and pass separately.

Wine suggestion: Medium white California wine

LA POÊLE D'OR

ADDRESS   1121 South Arlington Heights Road, Arlington
      Heights
TELEPHONE   593-9148
HOURS AND DAYS   Tues.–Thurs. 11:30 A.M.–2 P.M., 5–9 P.M.;
      Fri., Sat. 11:30 A.M.–2 P.M., 5–10 P.M.;
      Sun. 11:30 A.M.–8 P.M.
HOLIDAYS CLOSED   All major holidays
RESERVATIONS   No
CREDIT CARDS   No
ENTERTAINMENT   No
PARKING   Free
BANQUET FACILITIES   No
DRESS   Casual
LIQUOR   Yes
WINE   Limited selection

The decor is simple and the food is well prepared in this restaurant which specializes in a variety of omelettes and French crepes. Dinners come with fresh salad and French bread. Portions are extremely generous and priced reasonably. Favorites are the Campagnarde (tomatoes, garlic, mushrooms and spinach blended well together), and the Basquaise (shrimp with rice excellently combined with tomatoes, green peppers, and garlic). The cheesecake is a must for ending a delightful meal.

Crepe Ambassadeur

Serves 6

1 small onion, sliced
2 tablespoons oil
1½ pounds lean ground beef
1 cup precooked rice
4 fresh tomatoes, peeled and chopped
1 12-ounce can tomato purée
1 12-ounce can mushrooms

½ teaspoon salt
½ teaspoon thyme
½ teaspoon garlic powder
3 green peppers, chopped and sautéed in 2 tablespoons butter over low heat for 5 minutes
6 crepes (8"–9")
Parmesan cheese, grated

In skillet cook sliced onion in oil until brown. Add ground beef, break it up in chunks with a fork, and cook until brown. Pour off excess grease. Add cooked rice, tomatoes, tomato purée, mushrooms, salt, thyme, garlic powder and sautéed green peppers. Fill crepes with part of the filling; fold over. Mask them with the rest of the filling and sprinkle the cheese on top. Place under broiler for 1 minute before serving.

Wine suggestion: Medium red New York State wine

THE PRIME HOUSE

ADDRESS   4156 North Kedzie Avenue
TELEPHONE   463-9732
HOURS AND DAYS   Mon.–Fri. noon–midnight; Sat. noon–2 A.M.
HOLIDAYS CLOSED   Easter, Christmas, New Year's Day
RESERVATIONS   No
CREDIT CARDS   MC
ENTERTAINMENT   Organ, Fri.–Sun.
PARKING   Street
BANQUET FACILITIES   No
DRESS   Casual
LIQUOR   Yes
WINE   Limited selection

The Prime House is the neighborhood place for top-quality steaks and chops. Most entrees include "the largest baked potato in Chicago," rolls and complete salad bar. Their specialty, and a must to try is shish-ka-bob, made from beef tenderloin and cooked over an open hearth. The steaks are always outstanding and consistently cooked to perfection. Also available are delicious loin lamb chops. Dinners range from $6.50–$9.75 per person.

Shish-ka-bob

Serves 2

1½ *pounds beef tenderloin*
  Juice of 1 lemon
  Salt, to taste
  Pinch of oregano

2 *tomatoes*
2 *green peppers*
2 *small onions*

Season the meat with lemon juice, salt and oregano. Cut tomatoes and peppers into 1½″ squares, and quarter the onions. On long metal skewers, alternate the meat, onion, tomatoes and green peppers. Cook over an open hearth until meat reaches desired doneness.

Wine suggestion: Medium red California wine

THE PUMP ROOM

ADDRESS   1301 North State Parkway
TELEPHONE   266-0360
HOURS AND DAYS   Mon.–Thurs. 11:30 A.M.–midnight; Fri., Sat.
     11:30 A.M.–1 A.M.; Sun. 10 A.M.–midnight
HOLIDAYS CLOSED   Thanksgiving, Christmas
RESERVATIONS   Yes
CREDIT CARDS   AE
ENTERTAINMENT   Harpist in dining room; four-piece combo for
     dancing
PARKING   Valet service at hotel entrance
BANQUET FACILITIES   No
DRESS   Jacket for dining room; no jeans
LIQUOR   Yes
WINE   Extensive selection

The Lettuce Entertain You group changed their pace when they opened up the new and exciting Pump Room. The elegance of the original has been updated and vastly improved. A harpist playing soothing background music adds a unique and romantic touch. They also have a fantastic singer sitting near the dance floor, who can be easily heard from each table. The famous "booth one" still exists and is a sure place to find famous actors, authors and politicians. The enjoyable sight of women captains, dressed in fashionable black silk suits, emphasizes the modern trend of today. The curried crabmeat in avocado is a fabulous first course. If you're a soup lover, they occasionally offer cream of cauliflower soup. It's absolutely the best we've ever tasted. Fruits of the Sea (a seafood combination in sherry and cream) and the veal Calvados (veal and apples) were both delicious entrees. The desserts were outstanding. Everyone should try the Fudge Cake Bayonne and the Cheesecake Byfield.

Ratatouille

Serves 10

3–4 eggplants, peeled, cut
    lengthwise in half and
    then in quarters, seeded
    and sliced in ½" cubes
½ cup olive oil
  2 teaspoons Fruit-Fresh
    (ascorbic acid mixture)
  8 green peppers, cut in ½"
    cubes
  8 zucchini, cut in ½" cubes
  2 onions, peeled and cut in
    ½" cubes

  1 can plum tomatoes—
    remove seeds, save juice
  6 large cloves garlic, minced
  4 teaspoons salt
  1 tablespoon minced parsley
½ teaspoon thyme and 4
    large bay leaves, tied in a
    bag
  2 tablespoons sugar
1½ ounces lemon juice
  1 teaspoon baking soda
  1 cup Madeira

Sauté eggplant in oil and Fruit-Fresh about 2 minutes. Add remaining vegetables, garlic and salt, and cook on high heat 20–30 minutes. Add herbs, sugar, juice, soda and Madeira; cook 20–30 minutes more. Remove from heat, cool somewhat, remove bay leaves and thyme. Chill in non-metallic container at least 3 hours before serving. (It is even better made a day ahead.)

Wine suggestion: Rosé de Provence (France)

QUEEN OF THE SEA

ADDRESS   7611 South Stony Island Road
TELEPHONE   734-3030
HOURS AND DAYS   Mon.–Thurs. 11:30 A.M.–3 A.M.; Fri. 11:30
      A.M.–4 A.M.; Sat. 11:30 A.M.–5 A.M.; Sun. 1 P.M.–3 A.M.
HOLIDAYS CLOSED   Memorial Day, July 4, Christmas
RESERVATIONS   No
CREDIT CARDS   No
ENTERTAINMENT   No
PARKING   Yes
BANQUET FACILITIES   Yes
DRESS   Casual
LIQUOR   Yes
WINE   None
OTHER LOCATION   215 East 47th Street (624-1777)

     Queen of the Sea specializes in soul foods, although other types of dishes are available. They feature a buffet-style service for lunch and dinner. The buffet starts off with various salad selections. It includes at least three meat dishes—beef, pork and fried chicken. There are also barbecued ribs, ham hocks, oxtails and their outstanding specialty, short ribs of beef. The price of this extensive array of foods is only $2.95 for lunch and $3.95 for dinner. You're certainly encouraged to have "all you can eat." There are two banquet rooms for private parties. Off the main dining room is a service bar area, and there's a smaller dining room for a more intimate atmosphere.

Short Ribs of Beef

Serves 5

1 tablespoon dry mustard
5 tablespoons water
1 onion, finely chopped
1 clove of garlic, minced
1 tablespoon lemon juice
2 tablespoons wine vinegar
¼ cup olive oil

Salt and pepper to taste
1½ teaspoon chili powder
2 teaspoons cayenne
3 pounds lean short ribs of beef
2 tablespoons flour

Combine mustard and 2 tablespoons of the water; let stand for 10 minutes. Add onion, garlic, lemon juice, vinegar, olive oil, salt and pepper, chili powder and cayenne to mustard mixture. Pour over meat and refrigerate for at least 12 hours, turning occasionally. Drain. Preheat oven to 400°. Place meat in casserole with marinade in oven for 20 minutes. Lower heat to 350° and cook uncovered for 1 hour. Baste frequently. Add mixture of flour and 3 tablespoons water to thicken marinade and use for gravy.

Wine suggestion: French Hermitage or Chateauneuf du Pape, or California Petite Sirrah

REGAL COURT

ADDRESS   440 Greenbay Road, Highwood
TELEPHONE   433-6900
HOURS AND DAYS   Lunch: Tues.–Fri. 11:30 A.M.–2:30 P.M.
         Dinner: Tues.–Fri. 5–11 P.M.; Sat. 5 P.M.–1 A.M.; Sun.
         5–10 P.M.
HOLIDAYS CLOSED   Christmas
RESERVATIONS   Yes
CREDIT CARDS   AE, MC, VI
ENTERTAINMENT   No
PARKING   Yes
BANQUET FACILITIES   Up to 100
DRESS   Jacket
LIQUOR   Yes
WINE   Good selection

Discover a very nice, quiet, relaxing and intimate atmosphere here. Chef Joseph is charming. He came from Italy and has been cooking for 25 years. He opened this restaurant so more people could savor his distinctive cooking. Specialties of the house are Beef Wellington (filet of tenderloin wrapped in pastry crust), duck, stuffed trout, Veal Joseph and soft-shell crab. An extra treat is the homemade cheesecake. Service is very friendly and helpful.

Stuffed Ravioli with Cheese

Serves 10

FILLING

1 *pound ground veal*
½ *pound leaf spinach,*
  cooked
1 *onion*
1 *clove garlic*

2 *hard-boiled eggs*
  Salt and pepper to taste
  Pinch of nutmeg
¼ *cup bread crumbs*

Cook veal in a frying pan until done, then put through fine blade of a meat grinder with spinach, onion, garlic and eggs. Add salt and pepper, nutmeg and the bread crumbs and mix all the ingredients together.

DOUGH

3 *cups flour*
  Salt

5 *whole eggs*
  Chicken bouillon cubes

Mix flour, pinch of salt and eggs; knead the dough until shiny and elastic (about 10 minutes). Flour the table and stretch the dough out as thin as possible without breaking it. Cut the dough into 2″ squares. Put 1 tablespoon of the filling mixture on each of half the dough squares, cover with other half of the squares, and use a fork to press edges closed. Boil 2 gallons of water in a large pot; add salt and a few bouillon cubes for good taste. Cook the ravioli squares in batches. Boil each batch for 10 minutes. Take out and cool.

SAUCE

2 cloves garlic
¼ pound (1 stick) butter

1½ pounds mozzarella cheese, sliced

Sauté garlic cloves in butter; do not allow garlic to burn. Pour mixture through a strainer. Place filled ravioli squares in a casserole dish, pour sauce over, and cover with the mozzarella cheese. Bake for 10 minutes in a 450° oven.

Wine suggestion: Medium red Italian wine

LE RENDEZ-VOUS

ADDRESS   160 East Ontario Street
TELEPHONE   644-4240
HOURS AND DAYS   Lunch: Mon–Fri. 11:30 A.M.–2 P.M.
        Dinner: Daily 5:30–10:30 P.M.
HOLIDAYS CLOSED   All major holidays
RESERVATIONS   Yes
CREDIT CARDS   AE, MC
ENTERTAINMENT   No
PARKING   Doorman, at night only
BANQUET FACILITIES   For 60 to 70
DRESS   Jacket
LIQUOR   Yes
WINE   Extensive list

As the name implies, this restful, intimate restaurant is a good choice for a rendezvous. The feeling of warmth hits you immediately upon entering the main-floor bar and lounge area, and stays with you while dining in either of the two dining rooms. The upstairs area is plush, light and airy, in tones of blue and white with mirror accents. The downstairs decor is in earth tones, with bright 1920s Parisian oil paintings. Both eating areas create a quiet, private atmosphere with comfortable booths and soothing French background music.

The new French cuisine, a healthier approach to dining, is served here. It features lighter dishes, flourless sauces that are not overpowering and the use of sea salt and raw sugar only.

For lunch the ham and mushroom quiche was great and perfectly prepared. The smoked trout was delicate and served with a mild but satisfying horseradish sauce. The dishes we tried and recommend for dinner are the Dover Sole a La Roannaise, served with an excellent tasty vermouth sauce and chives, and the boneless chicken breasts with pears in a thin cream sauce.

231

All meals are served with a house salad and fresh vegetables. The chef makes his own outstanding pastries, which are displayed on a brass and glass pastry cart. By all means taste the strawberry cake. It's a heavenly experience and a perfect ending to a satisfying meal.

Poulet aux Poires "Pierre Hugo"

Serves 2

2 *boneless chicken breasts*
3 *tablespoons butter*
1 *cup white wine*
½ *cup mushrooms, sliced*
2 *pears, peeled and*
   quartered

2 *teaspoons shallots,*
   minced
1 *cup veal or chicken stock*
½ *cup heavy cream*
   Salt and pepper to taste

Sauté the chicken in 2 tablespoons of butter for about 7 minutes on each side or until brown. Set aside on heated platter. Deglaze pan with the wine. Add the shallots and mushrooms. Boil down for 1 minute. Add stock, cream and pears. Boil 5 minutes until sauce has thickened slightly. Stir in 1 tablespoon butter and salt and pepper to taste. Serve over chicken.

LA RESERVE

ADDRESS   6474 North Milwaukee Avenue
TELEPHONE   792-0660
HOURS AND DAYS   Lunch: Tues.–Fri. 11:30 A.M.–2:30 P.M.
      Dinner: Tues.–Fri. 5:30–10 P.M.; Sat. 5:30–11 P.M.;
      Sun. 4:30–9 P.M.
HOLIDAYS CLOSED   All major holidays
RESERVATIONS   Yes
CREDIT CARDS   AE, MC, VI
ENTERTAINMENT   No
PARKING   Yes
BANQUET FACILITIES   Up to 60 (exc. Mon. or Sat.)
DRESS   Jacket and tie; casual in bar
LIQUOR   Yes
WINE   Good selection

Chef-owner Henri Coudrier, former chef on the S.S. *France*, has turned his talents to this restaurant, winning awards such as *Holiday* magazine's 25th Anniversary Award and the Sons of Bacchus Award. His outstanding specialties include Baked Oysters Normande, Truite au Bleu (brook trout in white wine, cream and shallots), Les Cailles Grasses Aux Raisins (sautéed quail with grapes and Porto sauce), and fresh sea bass. La Reserve's central location makes it convenient to downtown, O'Hare Airport, and the North and Northwest suburbs. The menu is a la carte.

Filet de Boeuf
"Chevreuil" Grand Veneur

(How to prepare beef "venison" when venison is not available or is too expensive) Serves 8

3-pound beef tenderloin
   strip
2 carrots, sliced
2 medium onions, sliced
3 shallots, chopped
2 stalks celery, minced
   Parsley sprigs
¼ teaspoon thyme

2 bay leaves
1 tablespoon black
   peppercorns
4–5 cloves
   Mixture of 2 parts red
   wine, 1 part vinegar and 2
   parts oil—enough to cover
   meat

Place meat in a terrine and cover with a marinade of the remaining ingredients. Place in refrigerator for two weeks.

SAUCE GRAND VENEUR

Marinade (see above)
Oil
1 quart veal stock

3 tablespoons currant jelly
¼ cup cream

Remove meat from terrine and strain the marinade. Lightly sauté strained vegetables in oil. Add marinade liquid and cook until sauce is reduced by two-thirds. Add veal stock and cook 45 minutes. Strain the sauce again. Add the currant jelly and cream; stir to combine thoroughly.

DRESSAGE

Slice tenderloin in small tournedos (2 per person) and sauté to your preference. Serve on two round toasts sautéed in butter. Pour sauce over beef. Garnish the plate with chestnut purée, currant jelly and watercress. Serve fresh vegetables on side plate.

Wine: Medium red Burgundy, Rhone or California wine

THE RITZ-CARLTON
DINING ROOM

ADDRESS   160 East Pearson Street (Ritz-Carlton Hotel)
TELEPHONE   266-1000
HOURS AND DAYS   Luncheon: Mon.–Sat. noon–2:30 P.M.
      Dinner: Daily 6–11 P.M.
HOLIDAYS CLOSED   July 4
RESERVATIONS   Yes
CREDIT CARDS   AE, CB, DC, MC, VI, Marshall Field & Co.
ENTERTAINMENT   Yes
PARKING   Valet or self parking in Water Tower Place parking
      garage
BANQUET FACILITIES   Yes
DRESS   Jacket and tie
LIQUOR   Yes
WINE   Extensive selection

The original chef of the Paris Ritz was Auguste Escoffier. The Dining Room of the Ritz-Carlton Hotel of Chicago perpetuates the tradition of Escoffier and the Ritz by serving only the finest in classic French cuisine. The Dining Room reflects the charm and elegance of other Ritz Hotels throughout the world, with its French pine paneling and mirrored walls, Louis Quinze-style chairs, crystal chandeliers and intimate seating on raised platforms. The menu offers a large selection of interesting and superb dishes. Their Chateaubriand with Béarnaise Sauce and Bouquetière of Vegetables is outstanding. It is made for two people only. Also an excellent choice is the Truite Farcie en Berceau, stuffed trout with lobster mousse and champagne sauce. Their extensive menu is a la carte.

Creme d'Avocat Froid
(Cold Avocado Cream Soup)

Serves 12

¼ cup (½ stick) butter
3 tablespoons flour
1 teaspoon salt
½ teaspoon ground white
  pepper
1 quart chicken stock,

scalded (see below)
1 pint scalded whipping
cream
Juice of ½ lemon
2 medium avocados
Whipped cream for garnish

Melt butter in large saucepan, blend in flour, salt and pepper and whisk over low heat for 2 minutes. Add scalded chicken broth and cook, stirring, until mixture boils and thickens slightly. Add scalded cream and lemon juice. Heat to simmering; simmer for 15 minutes. Put into bowl and refrigerate until cold. Peel and seed avocados. Purée in electric blender with a small amount of cold soup. Blend into remaining soup base, stirring well. Serve in chilled cups. Garnish with a dab of whipped cream.

CHICKEN STOCK

2 pounds chicken necks and
  backs
2 quarts water
1 teaspoon salt
2–3 black peppercorns
2 leeks, chopped
2 stalks celery, chopped

1 carrot
1 onion, studded with 2
  cloves
4 sprigs parsley
1 bay leaf
½ teaspoon thyme

Place all ingredients in a large pot. Heat slowly to boiling. Skim surface, reduce heat, cover and simmer for 2–3 hours.
Wine suggestion: Entre-Deux-Mers or Mosel

R. J. GRUNTS

ADDRESS 2056 North Lincoln Park West
TELEPHONE 929-5363
HOURS AND DAYS Mon.–Thurs. 11:30 A.M.–midnight; Fri., Sat.
    11:30 A.M.–1 A.M.; Sun. 10 A.M.–midnight (Sun. brunch
    10 A.M.–2:30 P.M.)
HOLIDAYS CLOSED Thanksgiving, Christmas
RESERVATIONS No
CREDIT CARDS No
ENTERTAINMENT No
PARKING Reduced rate across the street
BANQUET FACILITIES No
DRESS Casual
LIQUOR Yes
WINE Limited selection

R. J. Grunts has a menu that's harder to put down than
some books we've read lately. It's creative, amusing and completely explanatory. It won an award from the National Restaurant Association as one of the top ten menus in the United
States in 1971. They have a terrific salad bar that never seems to
stop. It includes everything and then some. The soups, chili and
steaks are our favorites, accompanied by one of their unusual
house drinks.

Sorry Hun—No Bun

Serves 1

8 ounces ground beef
¼ cup Sorry Hun Topping
  (see below)
1 slice mozzarella cheese

2 slices beefsteak tomato
Your favorite Italian
dressing

Broil hamburger to desired doneness, then top with Sorry Hun Topping and cheese. Place under broiler just to melt cheese. Serve with tomato slices and dressing.

SORRY HUN TOPPING

¼ pound (1 stick) butter
1 green pepper, diced
½ large red sweet onion,
  diced
1 cup sliced mushrooms

½ teaspoon oregano
½ teaspoon basil
½ teaspoon salt
  Pinch black pepper
½ cup cherry tomato halves

Melt butter in a large skillet. Add green pepper, onion and mushrooms. Sauté briefly, until onions become slightly translucent. Add seasonings and toss gently. Just before removing from the fire, add cherry tomato halves. Keep warm for serving.
Wine suggestion: Medium red California wine

RON OF JAPAN

ADDRESS   230 East Ontario Street
TELEPHONE   644-6500
HOURS AND DAYS   Sun.–Thurs. 5–11:30 P.M.; Fri., Sat. 5 P.M.–
    12:30 A.M.
HOLIDAYS CLOSED   Thanksgiving
RESERVATIONS   Recommended
CREDIT CARDS   AE, DC, MC, VI
ENTERTAINMENT   No
PARKING   Yes
BANQUET FACILITIES   No
DRESS   Jacket required
LIQUOR   Yes
WINE LIST   Limited

Enter into the Japanese world of authentic Oriental art, music playing in the background and delicious odors of sizzling food. It's quite entertaining to watch the expert chefs prepare the food at tableside. Their showmanship is exhibited in their slicing, chopping and cooking to perfection. They offer complete dinners consisting of salad, soup, vegetables, rice, dessert and tea. We have particularly enjoyed the Crown Dinner, with which you get a shrimp appetizer topped with an egg yolk batter, steak (a choice of sirloin, filet or prime rib), and plum wine (a very sweet cordial). This dinner is priced at $12.50 per person. Also an excellent choice is the Lobster Boat Teppan-Yaki (lobster cooked and served in the shell).

Ron's Special Japanese Salad Dressing

About 2¾ cups

¼ *medium onion, grated*
1 *egg yolk*
   Dash of Tabasco Sauce

Dash of red pepper
2 *cups salad oil*
⅔ *cups soy sauce*

Combine all of the ingredients in a jar (1½-pint size or larger), shake well and serve over green salad of your choice.

SAGE'S EAST

ADDRESS   181 East Lake Shore Drive
TELEPHONE   944-1557
HOURS AND DAYS   Mon.–Thurs. 11 A.M.–1 A.M.; Fri., Sat.
   11 A.M.–2 A.M.
HOLIDAYS CLOSED   All major holidays
RESERVATIONS   Yes
CREDIT CARDS   All major cards
ENTERTAINMENT   From 5 P.M. to closing
PARKING   Doorman
BANQUET FACILITIES   Up to 200
DRESS   Jacket
LIQUOR   Yes
WINE   Good selection

     The solid wood decor and the intimate lighting add to the English atmosphere of Sage's East. They have a zesty menu of true Continental cuisine which lists the prices in pounds as well as in dollars. The main entrees are accompanied by an appetizer from the rolling carts, salad, potato and vegetables. Our personal favorite is the breast of duckling, rolled in coconut with a brandied cherry sauce. It's sweet, but great. Other dishes that we've tried and enjoyed are the rack of lamb and the stuffed lobster with crabmeat. Their Shrimp de Jonge, Gazpacho Soup, and Spinach Salad are all great beginnings to an enjoyable meal. The menu is extensive.

Rack of Lamb

Serves 4

2 *pounds rack of lamb*	*Salt and pepper*
Oil	*Rosemary*

Brush the rack of lamb with oil seasoned with salt and pepper. Bake in oven for 10 minutes at 400°, then turn it over, sprinkle with rosemary leaves and continue cooking for 10 more minutes. Serve with mint jelly and an assortment of prepared fresh vegetables.

Wine suggestion: Dry red Bordeaux

SEVEN EAGLES

ADDRESS   1050 Oakton Street, Des Plaines
TELEPHONE   299-0011
HOURS AND DAYS   Lunch: Mon.–Fri. 11:30 A.M.–3:30 P.M.
        Dinner: Mon.–Fri. 5–11 P.M.; Sat. 5–11:30 P.M.;
        Sun. noon–11 P.M. (dinner menu only)
HOLIDAYS CLOSED   None
RESERVATIONS   Accepted
CREDIT CARDS   All major cards
ENTERTAINMENT   Tues.–Sat.
PARKING   Free
BANQUET FACILITIES   Up to 400
DRESS   Jacket and tie
LIQUOR   Yes
WINE   Good selection

The decor of this restaurant combines old-world traditions with today's conventional living. It has three semi-circular dining rooms with booths and banquettes along the outer wall. The decorations are artistic, and the food is always superb. A visit to this restaurant would not be complete without at least a short stop in the Eagle's Nest Lounge. It is very intimate and appealing to all age groups. There is music to listen to or dance to Tuesday through Saturday evenings. The bartenders excel in mixing and preparing your favorite concoctions. If you feel in the mood to try something different, they are well qualified to suggest a new treat. You'll long remember your evening at Seven Eagles with nostalgia. For your dining enjoyment we suggest the Ladies' Strip Steak, Chicken Kalamata (with olive oil, lemon and oregano, the Athenian way), Stuffed Fresh Trout, Flaming Tenderloin Brochette, and Filets of Sole Marguery.

Calf's Liver Diane

Serves 3

3 tablespoons butter
4 tablespoons onion, sliced
  and chopped
2 slices Canadian bacon,
  each ⅛" thick
3 slices of calf's liver, each
  ¼" thick
  Freshly ground black
  pepper
  Salt

1½ ounces (3 tablespoons)
  Dubonnet wine
½ orange or 2 ounces (¼ cup)
  orange juice
4 ounces (½ cup) bordelaise
  sauce
1 teaspoon fresh parsley,
  chopped
1 ounce (2 tablespoons) dry
  brandy or cognac

Melt butter in a shallow pan and sauté onions for 2 minutes. Add the bacon and turn until partly brown on all sides. Add the liver and brown quickly on both sides. Season with fresh pepper and salt to taste. Pour wine over liver and simmer for 1 minute. Squeeze orange over liver (or pour juice over) and simmer for 1 minute more while constantly stirring. Pour the bordelaise sauce over the liver and stir while basting over liver. Sprinkle with parsley. Pour the brandy over and flame. When flame goes out, serve immediately with wild rice.

Wine suggestion: Dry red Bordeaux, California or New York State wine

SHANGHAI LIL'S

ADDRESS   5415 North Milwaukee Avenue
TELEPHONE   774-2600
HOURS AND DAYS   Opens Tues.–Sat. at 5 P.M., Sun. at 1 P.M.;
     closing times differ
HOLIDAYS CLOSED   Only those which fall on Mondays
RESERVATIONS   Not necessary
CREDIT CARDS   AE, CB, DC, MC, VI
ENTERTAINMENT   Yes
PARKING   Yes, in 4 lots
BANQUET FACILITIES   Yes
DRESS   Casual
LIQUOR   Yes
WINE   Limited selection

A lively Polynesian atmosphere pervades Shanghai Lil's at all times. Their famous Royal Hawaiian Revue takes place nightly on stage. The total happening convinces you that you're away on an authentic island vacation. Every Tues. and Sun. they offer a luau buffet filled with tasty selections. A few good ideas to order include the egg rolls, Shrimp Saigon (a flavorful sweet and sour dish), and Chicken Imperial (a dish of crisp breast of chicken on delicate bean sprouts). The side order of pork fried rice was great. The Mandarin Dinner for one can be ordered for $8.70 per person. This specialty includes 3 appetizers, soup, a choice among 5 entrees, dessert, fortune cookies and tea or coffee.

Shrimp Saigon

Serves 4

1½ pounds shrimp
½ cup flour
   Oil
2 eggs, beaten

Sweet and Sour Sauce (see below)
Sesame seeds

Shell, clean and devein fresh shrimp. Prepare batter, using flour, ¼ cup oil and eggs. Dip shrimp in batter and deep fry in oil until golden brown. Add to Sweet and Sour Sauce and serve over a bed of rice. Sprinkle with sesame seeds.

SWEET AND SOUR SAUCE

¼ cup vinegar
⅓ cup sugar
1 6-ounce can tomato paste
¼ teaspoon Chinese ginger
¼ clove garlic
   Juice of ½ lemon
   Tabasco Sauce

1½ cups pineapple chunks
1 large green pepper, seeded and diced
1 cup red grapes, seeded
2 tablespoons flour
¾ cup water

Bring the vinegar, sugar, tomato paste, ginger, garlic, lemon juice and Tabasco Sauce to a boil. When boiling, add pineapple, green pepper and grapes. Make a paste with the flour and water and add to thicken slightly.

Wine suggestion: Dry white Burgundy

SHRIMP WALK

ADDRESS   405 Sheridan Road, Highwood
TELEPHONE   432-0500
HOURS AND DAYS   Tues.–Thurs. 5–10 P.M.; Fri. 5–11 P.M.; Sat.
     4 P.M.–midnight; Sun. 4–9:30 P.M.
HOLIDAYS CLOSED   Thanksgiving, Christmas
RESERVATIONS   No
CREDIT CARDS   House card only
ENTERTAINMENT   No
PARKING   Yes
BANQUET FACILITIES   No
DRESS   Casual
LIQUOR   Yes
WINE   Limited house wines

A simple New Orleans touch is felt in the decor of the Shrimp Walk. They offer delicious fresh banana, strawberry and peach daiquiris. Start your meal with the onion soup served in a crock and topped with thick, chewy cheese. The restaurant's name means just what it implies, "Shrimp, the way you like it": order it butterflied, deep-fried or steamed in the shell with beer. King crab, dungeness crab and lobster are also available priced "at market." There are also hamburgers, fried chicken, and deep fried clams, all served in a basket with fries, cole slaw and pickle garnish. It's a cheerful place to go, stimulated by the friendly personalities of the owners, Sue and Bill Koretz.

Shrimps on Tap

Serves 6

2 quarts beer
2 tablespoons pickling spice
2 tablespoons All-Seasoning

3 pounds headless green
  shrimp in shell

Boil beer and spices. Add shrimp and bring to boiling again, for 3 minutes. Serve in juices, and offer a cocktail sauce on the side.
Wine suggestion: Sauvignon Blanc (dry white wine)

SLICKER SAM'S

ADDRESS   1911 Rice Street, Melrose Park
TELEPHONE   344-3660
HOURS AND DAYS   Mon.–Thurs. 11 A.M.–11 P.M.; Fri., Sat. 11
     A.M.–1:15 A.M.; Sun. 4–10 P.M.
HOLIDAYS CLOSED   Easter, Memorial Day, Labor Day,
     Christmas Eve, Christmas, New Year's Day
RESERVATIONS   6 or more
CREDIT CARDS   No
ENTERTAINMENT   No
PARKING   No
BANQUET FACILITIES   Weekdays only, up to 100
DRESS   Casual
LIQUOR   Yes
WINE   Limited house wines

Located in an unassuming building, Slicker Sam's serves marvelous Italian cuisine. The most creative expertise is spent on the seafood. Particularly exciting are the delicious baked oysters and clams, the crab legs, and the divine shrimp. The antipasto salad (lettuce, artichoke hearts, cheeses, cold meats) is fantastic. The pizza bread, eggplant, stuffed artichokes and bracciole (rolled butt steak) are all well prepared. Don't be discouraged by the long waits. The food is outstanding so it is worth it. A family-run place, Sam, Zena, Joe and Marianne are pleasant and make the dining more enjoyable.

Eggplant Parmesan

Serves 6

1 *large eggplant*	1 *clove garlic, minced*
2 *eggs*	1 *2-pound can Italian*
1½ *cups seasoned bread*	*tomatoes*
crumbs	1 *tablespoon onion, chopped*
½ *cup plus 3 tablespoons*	1½ *teaspoons dried basil*
grated Parmesan cheese	*leaves*
Fresh parsley, chopped	½ *pound mozzarella cheese,*
Salt and pepper	*sliced*
1 *cup olive oil*	

Peel, wash and cut eggplant crosswise into ¼″ thick slices. Place in layers on colander, sprinkling each layer lightly with salt. Place colander in a flat dish. Place a dish on top of eggplant and put a pot of water on the dish to force the liquid out of the eggplant. Let stand for 3 hours. Dry slices on absorbent paper. In a shallow bowl, beat eggs. Dip eggplant in eggs. Dredge in mixture of bread crumbs, ½ cup Parmesan cheese, 1 tablespoon chopped parsley, salt and pepper. Heat ¾ cup olive oil and sauté eggplant until golden brown on both sides. Drain on absorbent paper. In same saucepan, sauté onion and garlic in remaining ¼ cup oil until transparent. Add tomatoes, basil, and salt and pepper to taste, and cook 15 minutes, partially covered. Coat a 2-quart casserole with some of this sauce. Place some of the eggplant slices in a layer in casserole. Pour part of the sauce over the eggplant. Lay some of the mozzarella cheese over sauce. Continue these layers until all the ingredients are used up, ending with cheese. Sprinkle top with 3 tablespoons Parmesan cheese. Bake in preheated oven at 375° until the cheese melts. Garnish with parsley.

Wine suggestion: Dry red Italian wine

SU CASA

ADDRESS   49 East Ontario Street
TELEPHONE   943-4041
HOURS AND DAYS   Mon.–Fri. 11:30 A.M.–1 A.M.; Sat. 5 P.M.–2
     A.M.
HOLIDAYS CLOSED   All major holidays
RESERVATIONS   Yes
CREDIT CARDS   AE, CB, DC, VI
ENTERTAINMENT   Yes
PARKING   Doorman
BANQUET FACILITIES   Small groups
DRESS   Tie and jacket for dinner
LIQUOR   Yes
WINE   Limited selection

The decor at Su Casa sets the scene for an appropriate atmosphere by using original Mexican pieces dating from the sixteenth and seventeenth centuries. The authentic Mexican recipes are prepared with only the choicest of ingredients. The seasoning has purposely been modified for those who do not wish to eat highly spiced food, although the hotter accent condiments are available to suit your taste. The restaurant was selected by *Holiday* as one of Chicago's 10 best restaurants. They were also honored by Carte Blanche. We strongly recommend the Su Casa De-luxe Combination. The taste still lingers in our minds. It consists of carne asada, butterfly-cut beef tenderloin, chicken enchilada, cheese taco and several other outstanding items.

Trucha al Cilantro (Brook Trout with Fresh Coriander)

Serves 6

6 4–6-ounce boneless brook trout
3 ounces (6 tablespoons) lime juice
Salt and pepper to taste
6 ounces (¾ cup) flour
6 ounces (¾ cup) clarified butter

4 ounces (½ cup) cooking oil
2 cucumbers, cut lengthwise, seeded and sliced
3 teaspoons chopped fresh coriander

Sprinkle fish with 2 ounces (4 tablespoons) lime juice, salt and pepper. Flour on both sides. Heat large frying pan. Add 3 ounces (6 tablespoons) butter and the oil. Sauté fish, three at a time, until golden brown on both sides. Place on heated, greased baking sheet. Bake for 11 minutes at 350°. Heat small frying pan with remaining butter. Sauté cucumbers until clear and soft. Sprinkle with remaining lime juice and chopped coriander. Place fish on hot platter and arrange cucumbers over and around it.

Wine suggestion: Medium white California wine

SWEETWATER

ADDRESS   1028 North Rush Street
TELEPHONE   787-4081
HOURS AND DAYS   Daily 11:30 A.M.–2 A.M.
HOLIDAYS CLOSED   None
RESERVATIONS   Yes
CREDIT CARDS   All major cards
ENTERTAINMENT   No
PARKING   No
BANQUET FACILITIES   No
DRESS   Garden Room: Casual; Gourmet Room: No jeans
LIQUOR   Yes
WINE   Extensive selection

If you want to find the Rush Street crowd, this is the place. Sweetwater is located in the famous site of the old Mr. Kelly's. This restaurant-bar has a charming open feeling. You sit surrounded by windows, plants, and gentle tones of peaches and blues. There are two dining areas, the Gourmet Room and the more casual Garden Room. The Garden offers hamburgers, hot dogs, eggs, etc. The Gourmet caters to the more sophisticated tastes, offering Quenelles (dumplings of pike with lobster sauce), sweetbreads, boneless duck, Veal Piccata, rack of lamb, and, for desserts, mousse and soufflés.

Rock Cornish Hen

Serves 1

1 *Cornish hen, boneless*
  Salt and pepper
1 *tablespoon oil*
4 *tablespoons (½ stick)*
  butter
½ *teaspoon chopped shallots*
½ *teaspoon garlic*

½ *teaspoon tarragon*
1 *ounce (2 tablespoons)*
  cognac
¼ *cup dry white wine*
3 *tablespoons heavy cream*
½ *cup veal or chicken stock*
  Fresh parsley for garnish

Cut the hen open through the middle of the back and remove all bones. Season with salt and pepper. Put oil in ovenproof pan and let it get very hot. Add 2 tablespoons butter. Immediately add split hen skin side down, and let sizzle on both sides for 5 minutes per side. Put hen with juices in a 400° preheated oven for 10 minutes. Remove hen to a plate and discard grease. Add remaining 2 tablespoons butter, shallots, garlic and tarragon to pan and cook until shallots and garlic are golden brown. Put hen and cognac in pan and flame. Add wine and let it boil down for 1 minute. Remove hen. Separately add cream and then stock and let each boil down for 1 minute. Put hen in pan and let sizzle for 1 minute on each side. Put hen on plate, pour sauce over it and garnish with parsley.

Wine suggestion: Pinot Chardonnay

TANGO

ADDRESS   3172 North Sheridan Road
TELEPHONE   935-0350
HOURS AND DAYS   Lunch: Tues.–Sat. 11:30 A.M.–2:30 P.M.
    Dinner: Sun. 5:30–10:30 P.M.; Mon. 5:30–11 P.M.; Tues.–
    Thurs. 5:30–11:30 P.M.; Fri., Sat. 5:30 P.M.–12:30 A.M.
HOLIDAYS CLOSED   New Year's Day
RESERVATIONS   Yes
CREDIT CARDS   AE, MC, VI
ENTERTAINMENT   Occasionally
PARKING   Valet
BANQUET FACILITIES   Private parties
DRESS   Casual
LIQUOR   Yes
WINE   Good selection

Start off your "Tango" experience at the bar area. Trays of interesting hors d'oeuvres are displayed and available to stimulate your palate before dinner. The peaceful sight of a brightly lit aquarium is clearly in view behind the bar. For those romatically inclined, private booths are available, as well as two beautifully decorated dining rooms by the Barones. Soup and salad are included with each entree. The soup changes daily, but is generally excellent, and is served in white china soup tureens, left at your table for those tempted to have "seconds." The rack of lamb and king crab legs were our favorites.

Dover Sole en Croute

Serves 4

8 Dover sole fillets
1 fifth of white wine
Salt and pepper
MSG (monosodium glutamate)
Thyme
2 pounds fresh spinach

Pinch of baking soda
1 onion, diced
½ pound (2 sticks) butter
Nutmeg
4 cups puff pastry
1 egg yolk, lightly beaten

Poach sole in the wine, seasoned with salt, pepper, MSG and thyme. Cool. Flake apart with fork. Cook spinach, using a pinch of baking soda in the water to keep spinach green. Drain well, chop and sauté with onion in butter, adding small amounts of nutmeg, salt and pepper to taste. Cool. While fish and spinach are cooling, roll out half of puff pastry to ⅛" thick; cut into four 5" × 5" squares. Taking one square at a time, place about ¼ of the spinach on each piece of dough and about ¼ of the sole on top of each mound of spinach. Roll out the other half of puff pastry and cut as before. Brush around the edge of bottom pastry with egg yolk, place top pastry on and pinch the two together. Refrigerate until ready to use. Bake at 350° 10–15 minutes.

Wine suggestion: Dry white Burgundy

THAT STEAK JOYNT

ADDRESS   1610 North Wells Street
TELEPHONE   943-5091
HOURS AND DAYS   Mon.–Fri. 11:30 A.M.–2 A.M.; Sat. 4:30 P.M.–
   3 A.M.; Sun. 4 P.M.–1 A.M.
HOLIDAYS CLOSED   All major holidays
RESERVATIONS   Suggested
CREDIT CARDS   All major cards
ENTERTAINMENT   Piano bar
PARKING   2 hours free parking next door
BANQUET FACILITIES   From 20 to 300
DRESS   Casual
LIQUOR   Yes
WINE   Limited selection

Art, antique and history lovers come here, not only for
the good food, but to admire the decor—a restoration of the
Piper Bakery, which existed at the turn of the century. The
jeweled chandeliers and Tiffany lamps light the way to an impressive collection of antiques and rare "objets d'art." As the
name implies, the selections center around various cuts of beef.
The steaks can be ordered "your way," in a choice of char-
broiled, sautéed in onions, or broiled in garlic or peppercorns.
Also good is the pepper steak, sautéed with green peppers in
wine sauce.

Pepper Steak à la Paradise

Serves 8

2 *pounds mushrooms, diced*
2 *medium onions, diced*
1 *cup shallots, chopped*

2 *tablespoons garlic,*
   chopped
6 *green peppers, sliced*

1 cup (2 sticks) butter
  Demi-glace (see below)
2 cups red wine (Burgundy)
16 4-ounce slices of prime
  beef tenderloin

2 teaspoons salt
2 tablespoons black
  peppercorns, crushed

Sauté mushrooms, onions, shallots, garlic and green peppers in ½ cup (1 stick) butter in a saucepan until tender. Add demi-glace and wine. Season steaks with salt and crushed peppercorns. Pan-fry steaks in remaining ½ cup butter for 1 minute. Pour off excess butter. Bring the sauce to a boil and add to steaks. Serve immediately.

DEMI-GLACE

2½ pounds veal bones
 2 pounds meat trimmings
   (beef or veal)
 3 onions
 3 carrots
 1 stalk celery
 1 leek
 1 thyme leaf

1 bay leaf
1 gallon consommé or water
  Salt
½ cup brown roux made from
  ⅔ cup flour and 1 cup oil
  or grease from rendered
  beef fat

Chop bones small and cut up the trimmings. Coarsely dice vegetables. Brown together thoroughly in the oven. Place in a casserole. Add herbs, consommé or water, and a pinch of salt. Cook slowly for 24 hours. Add more water or consommé if liquid boils down too much. Boil down to 1 quart and strain. Add roux to this sauce and boil for 30 minutes. Keeps several days in refrigerator.

Wine suggestion: Medium red Burgundy

LE TITI DE PARIS

ADDRESS   2275 Rand Road, Palatine
TELEPHONE   359-4434
HOURS AND DAYS   Tues.–Fri. 11:30 A.M.–2:30 P.M., 5:30–
       10:30 P.M.; Sat. 5 P.M.–midnight; Sun. 3–11 P.M.
HOLIDAYS CLOSED   Christmas Eve, Christmas, New Year's Day
RESERVATIONS   Yes
CREDIT CARDS   MC, VI
ENTERTAINMENT   No
PARKING   Free
BANQUET FACILITIES   No
DRESS   Jacket
LIQUOR   Yes
WINE   Good selection

Le Titi de Paris, in French slang, means "the little rascal of Paris." Christian and Agnes add a special touch and provide authentic gourmet French cuisine with an elegant, intimate, and friendly atmosphere. Recommeded are the Crêpe aux Fruits de Mer (thin pancake filled with fresh seafood, in a light wine sauce), Steak au Poivre (steak sautéed with freshly ground pepper and flamed in cognac), Poitrine de Volaille Nantaise (boneless breast of chicken, fresh seafood sauce, cheese au gratin), Dover Sole d'Antin (sole braised in a white wine sauce, with fresh mushrooms and tomatoes), Medaillon de Veau Vallée d'Auge (thin scallopini of veal served with fresh apples) and, for dessert, the Chocolate Mousse. The attractive setting is created by the little lamps, linen tablecloths and napkins, fresh flowers and the French hand-painted china on the table.

Homard en Chemise

Serves 1

1 lobster tail
Salt, pepper and tarragon
to taste
1 tablespoon chopped
spinach seasoned with
pinch of salt, pepper,
nutmeg and 1 tablespoon
of half and half

1½ tablespoons mousse of
salmon, uncooked
9" x 9" flaky pastry dough,
⅓" thick
2 tablespoons butter
1 egg, beaten
Sauce (see below)

Take the meat from a fresh lobster tail out of its shell, leaving the tail end of the shell attached to the meat. Split the meat in the middle and sprinkle it with salt, pepper and a little tarragon. On one side lay the spinach, seasoned, chopped, and with as much water squeezed out as possible. On the other side put the mousse of salmon. After the lobster tail is well garnished with the spinach and the mousse of salmon, wrap it up in the flaky pastry dough; make sure the tail end of the shell is out. Put the prepared lobster on a buttered flat baking dish, smooth side up, brush a little beaten egg over the dough and bake in a preheated 400° oven until the crust is nice and brown. Serve with Sauce.

SAUCE

2 chopped shallots
4½ ounces (1 stick plus 1
tablespoon) butter
½ cup white wine

⅛ cup white-wine vinegar
Salt, white pepper, dash of
cognac to taste

Make sauce in a small pan. Cook shallots in 1 tablespoon of the butter for a few minutes. Add white wine and wine vinegar, reduce by one half and beat in 1 stick butter; season to taste.
Wine suggestion: Dry white Burgundy

TONY'S STEAK HOUSE

ADDRESS   2824 West Fullerton Avenue
TELEPHONE   342-8080
HOURS AND DAYS   Mon.–Fri. 11 A.M.–midnight; Sat. 2 P.M.–
    2 A.M.; Sun. 2–10:30 P.M.
HOLIDAYS CLOSED   None
RESERVATIONS   Yes
CREDIT CARDS   All major cards
ENTERTAINMENT   Yes
PARKING   Yes
BANQUET FACILITIES   No
DRESS   Casual
LIQUOR   Yes
WINE   Good selection

This fine Italian restaurant offers a menu to suit every-one's tastes. Begin your dinner by embarking on the small salad bar where everything (lettuce, tomatoes, cucumbers, onions, potato salad, etc.) is crisp and fresh. Enjoy entrees such as eggplant à la parmigiana, veal piccante, and beef bracciole (rolled butt steak), as well as a variety of their homemade pastas. Especially good is the fettuccine Alfredo with its rich cream and cheese sauce and a light touch of onions. The steaks are out-standing, cooked to perfection with crisp outsides and firm, pink insides. The casual and friendly atmosphere helps set the pace for a fun evening out.

Fettuccine Alfredo

Serves 4

8 ounces fettuccine noodles
¼ medium Spanish onion,
   chopped
½ pound (2 sticks) butter

⅔ cup cream
¼ pound (1¼ cups)
   Parmesan cheese, freshly
   grated

Cook noodles as directed on the box. Drain and return to pan. Sauté the onion in 1 tablespoon butter and add to the noodles. Toss all gently while adding the remaining butter, melted. Add the cream and allow to heat thoroughly, tossing once or twice, until most of the cream has been absorbed. Add the Parmesan cheese and continue tossing gently, until the noodles are evenly coated with the melted cheese. Serve immediately.
Wine suggestion: Medium white Italian wine

TOP OF THE HILTON

ADDRESS   Euclid Avenue & Rohlwing Road, Arlington Heights
(The Arlington Park Hilton)
TELEPHONE   394-2000
HOURS AND DAYS   Tues.–Thurs. 6 P.M.–midnight; Fri., Sat.
6 P.M.–1 A.M.; closed Sun. and Mon., except holidays
HOLIDAYS CLOSED   If holiday falls on Sun. or Mon., open for
dinner only
RESERVATIONS   Yes
CREDIT CARDS   All major cards
ENTERTAINMENT   Yes
PARKING   On premises
BANQUET FACILITIES   Yes
DRESS   Jacket and tie
LIQUOR   Yes
WINE   Good selection

This restaurant features headline entertainment, impeccable service and a breathtaking view of the area. Tues. through Sat., music is featured for dancing. On weekdays there is no cover charge; on Fri. and Sat. the charge is $3.00 per person. Recommended are the Steak Diane, New York sirloin steak, and Surf and Turf. This is a good place to dine before going to the theater downstairs.

Boneless Breast of Chicken

Serves 1

8 ounces boneless chicken breast	Salt and pepper
Flour	1 1-ounce slice ham
Paprika	2 stalks white asparagus
2 ounces (½ stick) butter	Pinch of parsley
1 tablespoon sherry wine	2 escarole leaves
½ cup medium cream sauce	3 kumquats

Coat chicken breast with flour seasoned with paprika. Sauté in ovenproof pan on both sides in all but 1 teaspoon of the butter until light brown—about 10 minutes. Bake in 300°–350° oven for 5 minutes. Remove breast from pan and keep at serving temperature. Place pan on top of range and simmer briefly to reduce moisture from fat; then deglaze with sherry wine. Add cream sauce and season to taste. Strain gravy and add remaining 1 teaspoon of butter. Keep at serving temperature. Place a slice of hot ham in the center of a dinner plate and cut to frame chicken breast. Place chicken breast on ham slice. Heat and then cut two white asparagus stalks into large pieces. Place on top of chicken breast. Pour sauce over chicken breast and sprinkle with chopped parsley. Garnish with escarole and kumquats.

Wine suggestion: Medium white Austrian wine

TOWER GARDEN AND RESTAURANT

ADDRESS   9925 Gross Point Road, Skokie
TELEPHONE   673-4450
HOURS AND DAYS   Lunch: Mon.–Sat. 11:30 A.M.–3 P.M.
        Dinner: Mon.–Fri. 5–10:15 P.M.; Sat. 5–11:15 P.M.;
        Sun. 3:30–9 P.M.
HOLIDAYS CLOSED   Memorial Day, July 4, Christmas, New
        Year's Day,
RESERVATIONS   Requested
CREDIT CARDS   AE, CB, DC, MC
ENTERTAINMENT   No
PARKING   Yes
BANQUET FACILITIES   Yes
DRESS   Jacket
LIQUOR   Yes
WINE   Extensive selection

Delicious food, an ambiance of sophistication, and intimacy can be found at this lovely restaurant. It is the winner of five consecutive *Holiday* Magazine Awards. Since 1968, the man in charge has been Reinhard Barthel, a graduate of the prestigious hotel management school in Lausanne, Switzerland. As managing director of the Tower, Barthel initiated a building and expansion program that brought the restaurant to its current stellar position on the dining scene.

Fine Continental cuisine is offered, along with wines from one of the largest and best equipped cellars in the country. Featured food items are rack of lamb with a bouquetière of vegetables, Fillet of Walleyed Pike Doria, and Truite au Bleu prepared with trout freshly netted from a tank of live fish. Many dishes are prepared at tableside, including Medallions of Venison, Hunter Style. During summer months, guests can dine outdoors in a delightful garden setting.

Walleyed Pike Doria

Serves 1

10–12 ounces fresh pike
   fillet
 ¼ teaspoon salt
 3 tablespoons lemon juice
 3 tablespoons Worcestershire
   sauce
 ½ cup flour
 ¼ cup (½ stick) butter

¼ medium diced, seeded,
   skinless cucumber
 1 tablespoon capers
   Few drops of dry white
   wine
 1 tablespoon chopped
   parsley

Marinate pike with salt, lemon juice and Worcestershire sauce for ½ hour. Dredge in flour. Sauté to golden brown in butter in skillet. Remove fish and put on platter. Sauté cucumbers and capers in butter remaining in pan, adding a few drops of wine. Add to fish. Sprinkle with chopped parsley. Garnish with lemon wedges. Serve with parsley boiled potatoes and the dry white wine used in cooking the fish.

Wine suggestion: Dry white Riesling (light-bodied dry white wine)

TRADER VIC'S

ADDRESS   17 East Monroe Street (Palmer House Hotel)
TELEPHONE   726-7500, ext. 385
HOURS AND DAYS   Mon.–Sat. 11:30 A.M.–1 A.M.; Sun. 4:30 P.M.–
     midnight
HOLIDAYS CLOSED   All major holidays
RESERVATIONS   Advisable
CREDIT CARDS   All major cards
ENTERTAINMENT   No
PARKING   Special rates after 5 P.M. at Mid-Continental Plaza
     (55 East Monroe)
BANQUET FACILITIES   Yes
DRESS   Jacket
LIQUOR   Yes
WINE   Limited selection

Enter into a South Sea Island setting to experience Polynesian or Continental cuisine. The extensive list of exotic rum drinks offered puts one in the appropriate mood. After trying several of their delicious appetizers, try one of their unusual specialties—Indonesian Lamb Roast, Peach Blossom Duck, or steak in flaming mustard sauce. Snowballs (vanilla ice cream, chocolate sauce and coconut) have always been a favorite dessert. The menu consists of eight pages listing an interesting variety of foods.

Bah Mee

Serves 4

½ pound white chicken meat
¾ pound prawns (of size 20–25 in a pound)
4 tablespoons peanut oil
1 tablespoon light soy sauce
¾ cup celery, julienne-sliced
¾ cup bamboo shoots, julienne-sliced
¾ cup Chinese pea pods, julienne-sliced

1 pound fresh Chinese egg noodles, cooked
6 dashes Tabasco Sauce
2½ cups chicken stock
2½ tablespoons bottled oyster sauce
¼ cup green onions, julienne-sliced
Salt to taste
1 tablespoon cornstarch

Cut chicken into ⅜"-thick pieces and sauté with prawns in oil until they start to turn color. Add soy sauce and stir. Add celery, bamboo shoots and pea pods; stir quickly for 10 seconds. Add noodles and Tabasco Sauce and stir until all ingredients are completely mixed. Add chicken stock and bring to boiling for 1–2 minutes. Add oyster sauce, green onions, salt and cornstarch mixed with ¼ cup water. Cook until slightly thickened.

Drink suggestion: Powerful rum drink

TRATTORIA GALLO

ADDRESS   6755 North Cicero Avenue, Lincolnwood
TELEPHONE   679-0133
HOURS AND DAYS   Lunch: Mon.–Fri. 11 A.M.–2:30 P.M.
          Dinner: Nightly 4 P.M.–midnight
HOLIDAYS CLOSED   Christmas
RESERVATIONS   Accepted
CREDIT CARDS   AE, MC, VI
ENTERTAINMENT   Yes
PARKING   Yes
BANQUET FACILITIES   No
DRESS   Casual
LIQUOR   Yes
WINE   Good selection

Glenna Syse, theater critic for the Chicago *Sun Times*, strongly recommended this lively suburban spot. She was right. They have an excellent salad bar with countless antipasto items. These unlimited selections come with your entree, as do freshly made bread, soup, pasta and dessert. The good service and delicious Italian cuisine make this restaurant a popular favorite among the suburban and city crowds. Two great veal dishes that we tried were the Piccanti di Milano (veal and mushrooms, sautéed in lemon and butter) and the veal cutlet with eggplant, baked in a mozzarella cheese and tomato sauce. The pasta selection offers a large variety of outstanding choices.

Chicken a la Lucia

Serves 4

4 *boneless breasts of chicken*	1 *cup olive oil*
Flour	3 *tablespoons butter*
3 *eggs*	¼ *cup mushrooms, chopped*
Parmesan cheese	¼ *cup sherry*
Parsley, chopped	2 *cloves garlic, minced*
Salt and pepper to taste	*Mozzarella cheese*

Dredge chicken in flour and dip in egg batter made from eggs, Parmesan cheese, parsley and salt and pepper to taste. Fry in oil until golden brown. Drain off oil completely. Place butter in frying pan and sauté mushrooms with sherry. Season to taste with salt, pepper, parsley and garlic. Top with the mozzarella cheese. Simmer 10–15 minutes.

Wine suggestion: Medium white Italian wine

TRUFFLES

ADDRESS   151 East Wacker Drive (Hyatt Regency Chicago
   Hotel)
TELEPHONE   565-1000
HOURS AND DAYS   Lunch: Mon.–Fri. 11:30 A.M.–2:30 P.M.
   Dinner: Mon.–Sat. 6–11 P.M.
HOLIDAYS CLOSED   All major holidays
RESERVATIONS   Yes
CREDIT CARDS   All major cards
ENTERTAINMENT   No
PARKING   Indoor parking
BANQUET FACILITIES   No
DRESS   Jacket
LIQUOR   Yes
WINE   Extensive selection

Truffles has an atmosphere that's modern, sleek and elegant in rich rust and black tones. The food is equally elegant. Listed under the hors d'oeuvres is the Truffles en Croute—Sous la Cendre, a whole truffle baked in a crust. It's an extraordinary dish which is rarely found in the Chicago area, with an extraordinary price of $14. The Scotch Salmon was served delicately thin and proved to be an excellent first course. The impressive presentation of each entree added to the total dining experience. The rack of lamb was served with a tasty potato basket. The duck was delicious and was served with wild rice and bacon. The tornedos were excellent and served with a perfectly seasoned béarnaise sauce. Each entree included a side dish of interesting fresh vegetables cooked at the table. For dessert, their scrumptious chocolate soufflé is a must. After-dinner drinks are brought to your table on a portable bar. An added touch that we enjoyed was the sculptured birds made from lard, placed around the room.

Soufflé au Chocolat

Serves 4

1 *ounce (2 tablespoons)
  butter*
1 *ounce (2 tablespoons) flour*
3 *ounces (6 tablespoons)
  sugar*
7 *fluid ounces milk*

½ *teaspoon vanilla extract*
¼ *pound semi-sweet
  chocolate*
5 *egg yolks*
4 *stiffly beaten egg whites*

Melt the butter. On the side, mix the flour and sugar together. Boil the milk and, while boiling, add the vanilla, then the flour-sugar mixture and butter. Heat mixture until it thickens (about 5 minutes), then remove from heat. Melt chocolate and pour into the mixture. Whip egg yolks and add them. Then fold stiffly beaten egg whites into the mixture by hand. Pour entire mixture into buttered and sugared 5-cup soufflé dish. Set casserole into flat pan filled with approximately ⅛" tap water. Cook in pre-heated oven set at 375° for 30 minutes, or until baked "dry."
Wine suggestion: Sweet white Bordeaux

THE WATERFRONT

ADDRESS   1015 North Rush Street
TELEPHONE   943-7494
HOURS AND DAYS   Mon.–Thurs. 11:30 A.M.–midnight; Fri., Sat.
      11:30 A.M.–1 A.M.; Sun. 11:30 A.M.–11 P.M.
HOLIDAYS CLOSED   None
RESERVATIONS   Recommended
CREDIT CARDS   AE, VI
ENTERTAINMENT   No
PARKING   No
BANQUET FACILITIES   No
DRESS   Casual—no T-shirts or cutoffs
LIQUOR   Yes
WINE   Limited selection

Dim lights and copper tabletops give The Waterfront a warm and cozy feeling. The nautical decor is enhanced when you pass the fresh lobster swimming in the tank. The waiters are alert and friendly. The salad bar is superb. Everything is crisp and fresh. There are clam bakes on Sunday and a fresh fish catch every day. Dungeness crab, Sole en Saque, Alaskan king crab and the tiny bay scallops are of good quality and well prepared.

Sole en Saque

Serves 4

1 *tablespoon chopped shallots*	1 *cup tiny shrimp*
1 *tablespoon chopped onions*	2 *tablespoons chopped olives*
2 *tablespoons butter*	*Salt, pepper, mace and thyme to taste*
2 *tablespoons flour*	8 *fillets of sole*
1 *cup warm milk*	4 *thin slices of ham*
2 *ounces (¼ cup) sherry*	4 *oiled paper bags*

Sauté shallots and onions in butter. Stir in flour and milk; stir constantly until sauce thickens. Add sherry, shrimp and olives. Season to taste and set aside to cool. Place a fillet of sole on a slice of ham. Spoon on cooled sauce and cover with a second fillet, place another spoonful of sauce on top and, using a spatula, slip creation into oiled paper bag. Close and crimp end of bag and place on greased cookie sheet in 375° oven for 25 minutes. Serve with piping hot rice pilaf and crackling cold Chablis.
Wine suggestion: California or French Chablis

ZWEIG'S RESTAURANT AND DELICATESSEN

ADDRESS   8630 Golf Road, Des Plaines
TELEPHONE   297-4343
HOURS AND DAYS   Sun.–Thurs. 6 A.M.–1 A.M.; Sat. 24 hours
HOLIDAYS CLOSED   None
RESERVATIONS   No
CREDIT CARDS   No
ENTERTAINMENT   No
PARKING   Yes
BANQUET FACILITIES   No
LIQUOR   No

As you enter Zweig's Deli, your appetite is immediately aroused by the aroma of the kosher-style corned beef, delectable pastrami, juicy dill pickles, fresh Jewish rye bread and a variety of rolls. It's a great place for hot dogs, hamburgers, turkey, caviar and chopped-liver sandwiches. The homemade chicken soup with kreplach or matzo balls, the mushroom barley soup and the borscht are delicious. This is a family owned and operated restaurant that has been in business since 1919. It is across the street from the Mill Run Theater, so the celebrities appearing there frequent this restaurant, and you often have the pleasure of seeing them. The restaurant has a dining room as well as a "carry-out" service.

Sauté Jumbo Shrimp

Serves 4

1 *pound shrimp*	*Pinch garlic powder*
1 *cup flour*	2 *tablespoons butter or*
1 *teaspoon seasoned salt*	*cooking oil*
Pinch white pepper	*Lemon*

Clean and devein shrimp. Mix together the shrimp, flour, salt, pepper and garlic. Heat butter in frying pan and brown shrimp on both sides. Drain butter and reserve. Put shrimp on toast points; pour reserved butter over. Serve with lemon slices.

Wine suggestion: Dry white Loire wine

SHORT TAKES

ARMANDO'S   100 East Superior   337-7672
>Consistently good Italian cuisine

THE BAGEL   4806 North Kedzie   463-7141
>Quite small, but marvelous homemade Jewish food

BANGKOK HOUSE   2544 West Devon   338-5948
>Inexpensive, tasty and unusual Thai-style cuisine

BARNEY'S MARKET CLUB   741 West Randolph   263-9795
>A great place for lobster

BARONE'S   401 West Armitage   266-7337
>A large selection of Italian dishes; fresh homemade bread

BATT'S MAMA RESTAURANT   112 East Cermak Road
842-7222
>Hefty corned beef sandwiches and great brisket dinners

BENGAL LANCERS   2324 North Clark   929-0500
>Delicious selection of curries and chutneys; fantastic appetizers

BINYON'S   327 South Plymouth Court   341-1155
>Good German and American cuisine in downtown area

BLACK FOREST   2636 North Clark   348-7930
>An extensive menu of German cuisine in an authentic decor

BYRON   2628½ West Touhy   743-7050
>$13.95 includes soup to dessert of satisfying French cuisine; bring your own wine

CAFE LA CAVE   2733 Mannheim Road, Des Plaines   827-7818
>Good French food; convenient to O'Hare Airport

CAFE DE PARIS   1260 North Dearborn   943-6080
>Outstanding spot for duck lovers

THE CART   601 South Wabash   427-0700
>Excellent prime ribs, steaks, ribs, french-fried shrimp, etc.

CAS AND LOU'S   3457 West Irving Park   588-8445
>Delicious Italian dishes at very reasonable prices

CESAR'S   18601 Cicero, Country Club Hills   957-0900
>Very tasty Italian cuisine

CHARLIE BEINLICH'S   290 Skokie Boulevard, Northbrook   No phone
>Order a shrimp cocktail and one of their hamburgers

LA CHOZA   7630 North Paulina   465-9401
>A large selection of inexpensive, tasty Mexican food

COMEBACK INN   1913 Lake, Melrose Park   343-7490
       A great hamburger spot
COUNTRY SQUIRE   at junction of Ill. Hwy. 120 and U.S. Hwy.
45, Grayslake   223-0121
       A family place, American food
DAE HO   2741 West Devon   274-8499
       Outstanding Korean food at reasonable prices
EL INCA   6221 North Broadway   465-9647
       A delicious Peruvian menu that changes each day
EMBERS   67 East Walton   944-1105 or 1034 North
Dearborn   664-1458
       Excellent prime rib at two locations
L'EPUISETTE   21 West Goethe   944-2288
       Superb variety of seafood
LES FONTAINES ROUGES   1011 West Irving Park   327-2770
       Moderate prices for good food and elegant atmosphere
FRENCH PORT   2585 North Clark   528-6644
       A great spot specializing in fresh seafood
THE GALLERY   194 East Westminster, Lake Forest   234-0770
       Delightful food with an attractive artwork setting
GARDEN OF HAPPINESS   3450 North Lincoln   348-2120
       Great Korean dishes
GENNARO'S   1352 West Taylor   243-1035
       Delicious homemade pasta and pizza
GINO'S EAST   160 East Superior   943-1127
       Excellent pizza in the pan
GIORDANO'S   6253 South California   436-2969
       Outstanding double-crusted thick pizza
GLADYS' LUNCHEONETTE   4527 South Indiana   548-6848
       Delicious soul food—especially the chicken, biscuits and
       desserts
GORDON   512 North Clark   467-9780
       Continental menu that changes daily
HACKNEY'S   1514 East Lake, Glenview   273-4485 or 1241
Harms, Glenview   724-5577
       Great hamburgers on black bread, onion rings
HALF SHELL   676 West Diversey   549-1773
       Super seafood at moderate prices
HAMBURGER HAMLET   44 East Walton   649-6600
       Watch them grind *tenderloin* in front of you; great oyster bar
HEARTHFARE   1918 Waukegan Road, Glenview   724-3830
       Consistently delicious food

HOME RUN INN   4254 West 31st Street   247-9696
      Excellent thin-crust pizza made from the finest ingredients
HOUSE OF HUNAN   3150 North Lincoln   327-0427
      Outstanding Mandarin, Hunan and Szechuan dishes
HUGO'S   800 North Michigan   649-0345
      A pleasant dining spot with a view of the famous Water Tower
JACQUES' FRENCH RESTAURANT   900 North Michigan
944-4795
      A European garden setting with fine food
KIYO'S   2827 North Clark   935-0474
      Sensational setting with Japanese cuisine
MAISON MICHELE   2118 North Clark   281-9659
      Not fancy, but fabulous French food
MARTINI'S   232 West Grand   337-2935
      Low prices for good Italian-American food
THE MAVIN   701 North Michigan   337-1717
      New version of the old famous Fritzel's
MEDITERRANEAN HOUSE   3910 Dempster, Skokie   679-7222
      Serve yourself with Middle Eastern cuisine
MELVIN'S   1116 North State   664-0356
      Fabulous and popular outdoor cafe—inside, the same tasty
      food
THE MEZZANINE   Water Tower Place, 835 North Michigan
649-1100
      Two separate eating experiences of interesting foods: a sit-
      down and a help-yourself
MIDDLE EASTERN GARDENS   2621 North Clark   935-3100
      Delicious specialty is falafel and pita bread
MILLER'S STEAK HOUSE   7011 North Western   743-3333
      Fabulous ribs that are well worth the wait
MIOMIR'S SERBIAN CLUB   2255 West Lawrence   784-2111
      Lively European cafe setting; French, American and
      Yugoslavian food
MON PETIT   1255 North State   944-1383
      Fine French cuisine; features late-night menu
MUSHROOM AND SONS, LTD.   1825 Second Street, Highland
Park   432-0824
      Great salads and sandwiches
NANCY'S   7309 West Lawrence, Harwood Heights   867-4641
      Stuffed pizza and homemade pastas
NORTH STAR INN   15 West Division   337-4349
      Fantastic steak sandwich; good late-night suggestions

OAK TREE   25 East Oak   751-1988
        Sandwiches or eggs 24 hours a day, 7 days a week
THE OTHER SIDE   2300 Lincoln Park West   525-7375
        Good ribs and cabbage soup; next to Al Farber's
PEKING DUCKLING HOUSE   2045 West Howard   338-2016
        Excellent Mandarin cuisine—call ahead to order the
        "Presidential Dinner"
PUNCHINELLO'S   936 North Rush   642-3106
        Fabulous sandwiches and spontaneous entertainment
        nightly—great fun
SAM MEE   3370 North Clark   525-5050
        Large selection of good Korean food
SAN PEDRO   Plaza Del Lago, Wilmette   251-6621
        Good place for lunch; great hot cinnamon rolls
THE SILO   625 Rockland Road, Lake Bluff   234-6660
        A place to enjoy super, thick-crust pizza
SQUASH BLOSSOM,   2350 North Clark   929-5500
        Varied menu in pleasant surroundings
TAJ MAHAL   10 East Walton   642-7446
        Well-prepared Indian cuisine in intimate surroundings
TOWN AND COUNTRY   5970 North Ridge   334-5345
        Consistently good; great bakery for delicious treats to take
        home
VALLEY LODGE   2132 Waukegan, Glenview   724-7440
        Tasty gyro sandwiches and hamburgers
VILLAGE TAVERN   Old McHenry Road, Long Grove
634-3117
        A fun place, auction in the evenings; chicken, ribs and
        sandwiches
WALKER BROS. ORIGINAL PANCAKE HOUSE   153 Green
Bay, Wilmette   251-6000
        Greatest apple pancake in the world; great variety of pancakes
WARSAW RESTAURANT   820 North Ashland   666-3052
        Excellent Polish cuisine—tasty dumplings and Hunter's Stew
WING HOE   5356 North Sheridan   275-4550
        Friendly service and outstanding Cantonese food
WING YEE'S   2556 North Clark   935-7380
        A popular spot for Cantonese cuisine
WRIGLEY BUILDING RESTAURANT   410 North Michigan
944-7600
        Well-prepared American cuisine
YU-LIN'S CHINESE DUMPLING HOUSE   1636 Old Deerfield,

Highland Park   831-3155
      Good food; order the Mongolian Pot ahead of time
ZAVEN'S   260 East Chestnut   787-8260
      A wide variety of interesting and superb food
ZLATA'S BELGRADE RESTAURANT   1516 North
Milwaukee   252-9514
      Excellent Serbian food with friendly, warm atmosphere

RECIPE INDEX

APPETIZERS

Chicken Liver Pâté (Court House)
Coquilles St. Jacques aux Petite Legumes (Maxim's de Paris)
Coquilles St. Jacques "Provençale" (Jovan)
Eli's Chopped Liver (Eli's, The Place for Steaks)
Glazed Chicken Liver Pâté (The Indian Trail)
Guacamole (Meson del Lago)
Kamoosh Appetizer (Cafe Azteca)
Oysters J.W. (King's Wharf)
Saganaki (Flaming Cheese) (Dianna's Restaurant Opaa)

BEEF ENTREES

Authentic Sukiyaki (Dai-Ichi)
Beef Back Ribs (Eugene's)
Beef Colbert (Four Torches)
Beef Wellington (Beverly House)
Braised Short Ribs of Beef (Oscar's)
Burger au Cricket (Cricket's)
Carbonnades Flamande (Le Festival)
Crêpe Ambassadeur (La Poêle d'Or)
Entrecôte Marchand de Vin (Ile de France)
L'Entrecôte Orientale (The Consort)
Filet de Boeuf "Chevreuil" Grand Veneur (La Reserve)
Hungarian Beef Goulash (Epicurean)
Kahala Beef (Kahala Terrace)
Pepper Steak (Myron and Phil's Steak and Lobster House)
Pepper Steak a la Paradise (That Steak Joynt)
Pickled Beef (Klas)
Sauerbraten (Brown Bear Restaurant)
Sauerbraten, Dumplings and Gravy (Ignatz and Mary's Grove Inn)
Shish-Ka-Bob (The Prime House)
Short Ribs of Beef (Queen of the Sea)
Sirloin Steak Arnie's (Arnie's)

LAMB ENTREES

PASTA

PHEASANT ENTREE *see* POULTRY ENTREES

PORK ENTREES

"The Cottage" Schnitzel (The Cottage)
Dr. Shen's Barbecued Spareribs (The Abacus)
Pork in Wine Sauce (Candlelight Dinner Playhouse)
Scutzafarno Pizza Sausage Sandwich (The Brassary)

POULTRY ENTREES

Chicken
Bah Mee (Trader Vic's)
Boneless Breast of Chicken (Top of the Hilton)
Chicken Coconage (Jasand's)
Chicken Coral Sea (Kon-Tiki Ports)
Chicken Kalakala (Fu-Lama Gardens)
Chicken a la Lucia (Trattoria Gallo)
Chicken Vesuvio (Gene and Georgetti's)
Enchiladas Suizas (Mi Casa-Su Casa)
Malnati Chicken (Lou Malnati's Pizzeria)
Petti di Pollo alla Strozzi (Italian Village, The Florentine Room)
Poulet au Curry (The Barn of Barrington)
Poulet Florentine (La Cheminée)
Poulet aux Poires (Le Rendez-Vous)
Szechuan Diced Chicken (Dragon Inn North)

Duck
Duck a la Grassfield's (Grassfields International Restaurant)
Roast Duck (Cafe Bohemia)
Roast Long Island Duckling a la Maison (Hans' Bavarian Lodge)
Roast Wisconsin Duckling, Bigarade Sauce (Camellia House and
   Terrace Lounge)

Hen
Rock Cornish Hen (Sweetwater)

Pheasant
Roast Pheasant with Wild Rice Dressing (The Milk Pail)

Squab
Squabs with Sausage and Sauerkraut (Le Perroquet)

SQUAB ENTREE *see* POULTRY ENTREES

SALADS

Blackhawk Salad (The Blackhawk)
Ron's Special Japanese Salad Dressing (Ron of Japan)
Salade Niçoise (Café Metropole)
Special Salad (Pizzeria Due)
Waldorf Salad (Fritz, That's It!)

SANDWICH

Scutzafarno Pizza Sausage Sandwich (The Brassary)

SAUCES

Claim Sauce (Chicago Claim Company)
Ginger Sauce (Benihana of Tokyo)
Mornay Sauce (Mel Markon's Zanadu)
Teriyaki Sauce (Ichiban of Chicago)

SEAFOOD ENTREES *see* FISH AND SEAFOOD ENTREES

SOUPS

Al Farber's Famous Cabbage Soup (Al Farber's Steak Room)
Bisque Champignon (Mushroom) (The Left Bank)
Bisque de Homard Robert (Lobster) (Le Francais)
Cheese Soup (The Great Gritzbe's Flying Food Show)
Clam Chowder (Jonathan Livingston Seafood)
Creme d'Avocat Froid (Cold Avocado) (The Ritz-Carlton Dining Room)
Danish Holiday Soup (Nielsen's)
Hot Sweet and Sour Cabbage Soup with Short Ribs (Mel Markon's)

VEAL ENTREES

Breaded Veal Cutlet Parmesan (Febo)
Calf's Liver Diane (Seven Eagles)
Costoletta Valtostana (Stuffed Veal Chops) (Doro's)
Gschnaetzlets (Veal) (Berghoff Restaurant)
Veal Oscar a la Waldorf (The Atrium)
Veal en Papillote (Plentywood Farm)
Veal Picante (Chef Alberto's)

LOCATION INDEX

Bullets (•) indicate restaurants listed in the Short Takes section.

CITY

Loop Area
- • Barney's Market Club
- Berghoff Restaurant
- • Binyon's
- The Blackhawk
- Cafe Bohemia
- • The Cart
- Dai-Ichi
- Dianna's Restaurant Opaa
- Epicurean
- Gene and Georgetti's
- Greek Islands
- Italian Village (The Florentine Room)
- La Margarita
- • Martini's
- Trader Vic's
- Truffles

West Side
- • Bangkok House
- • Cas and Lou's
- • Gennaro's

South Side
- • Batt's Mama Restaurant
- Beverly House
- Court House
- Febo
- • Giordano's
- • Gladys' Luncheonette
- • Home Run Inn
- Lee's Canton Cafe
- Queen of the Sea

Near North Side
- • Armando's
- Arnie's
- Benihana of Tokyo

- The Brassary
- Cafe Azteca
- • Cafe de Paris
- Camellia House and Terrace Lounge
- Cantonese Cafe
- Cape Cod Room
- La Cheminée
- Chez Paul
- Consort Room
- Cricket's
- Dingbat's
- Doro's
- Eli's, The Place for Steak
- • Embers
- • L'Epuisette
- Eugene's
- Le Festival
- Gaylord India Restaurant
- • Gino's East
- • Gordon
- The Great Gritzbe's Flying Food Show
- • Hamburger Hamlet
- Hotspur's
- • Hugo's
- Hy's of Chicago
- Ireland's
- • Jacques'
- Jasand's
- Jovan
- Kon-Tiki Ports
- Lawry's The Prime Rib
- The Magic Pan Creperie
- • The Mavin
- • Melvin's
- Meson del Lago

LOCATION INDEX

SUBURBAN LISTINGS

290

LOCATION INDEX

CUISINE INDEX

Bullets (•) indicate restaurants listed in the Short Takes section.

ARMENIAN

Casbah II
- Mediterranean House
- Middle Eastern Gardens

ASSORTED GOURMET

Beverly House
- Binyon's
The Blackhawk
- Country Squire
Dingbat's
- The Gallery
- Hamburger Hamlet
Homestead

Jasand's
- The Mezzanine
The Milk Pail
- Mushroom and Sons, Ltd.
Nite-N-Gale
- North Star Inn
Plentywood Farm

- San Pedro
- The Silo
- Squash Blossom
- Town and Country
- Valley Lodge
- Village Tavern
- Wrigley Building Restaurant

BOHEMIAN

Klas

BRUNCHES, SUNDAY

Arnie's
The Atrium
- The Bagel
Camellia House and Terrace Lounge
Court House
Cricket's

Four Torches
Fritz, That's It!
Grassfield's International Restaurant
The Great Gritzbe's Flying Food Show
Hotspur's

Jonathan Livingston Seafood
Mel Markon's
The Milk Pail
Les Oeufs
The Pump Room
R. J. Grunts

CANTONESE

The Abacus
The Bird
Cantonese Cafe

Fu-Lama Gardens
Lee's Canton Cafe
- Wing Hoe

- Wing Yee's

CONTINENTAL

Allgauer's Fireside
Arnie's
The Atrium
The Bakery
The Barn of Barrington
Cafe Bohemia
Café Metropole
Camellia House and
   Terrace Lounge
Chef Alberto's
The Connoisseur's
   Dining Room
The Consort
The Cottage

Country Inn of
   Northbrook
Court House
Cricket's
Eugene's
Farmer's Daughter
• Les Fontaines Rouges
Four Torches
• Gordon
Grassfield's Inter-
   national Restaurant
• Hearthfare
• Hugo's
Hy's of Chicago

• The Mavin
• Miller's Steak House
Nielsen's
The Ninety-Fifth
The Pump Room
Regal Court
Sage's East
Seven Eagles
Sweetwater
Top of the Hilton
Tower Garden and
   Restaurant
• Zaven's

CREPES AND EGGS

La Creperie
The Magic Pan

Creperie
Les Oeufs

La Poêle d'Or

DINE AND DANCE

Arnie's
Camellia House and
   Terrace Lounge

The Consort
Maxim's de Paris
The Pump Room

Top of the Hilton

DINNER AND THEATER

Candlelight Dinner
   Playhouse

FRENCH

Le Bon Vivant
• Byron
• Cafe La Cave
• Cafe de Paris
La Cheminée
Chez Paul
Le Festival
Fond de la Tour

La Fontaine
Le Francais
Ile de France
• Jacques'
Jovan
The Left Bank
Maxim's de Paris
• Mon Petit

Le Perroquet
Le Rendez-Vous
La Reserve
The Ritz-Carlton
   Dining Room
Le Titi de Paris
Truffles

GERMAN

Berghoff Restaurant
• Black Forest

Brown Bear
Hans' Bavarian Lodge

Ignatz and Mary's
   Grove Inn

GREEK

Dianna's Restaurant
   Opaa

E'La Cum Inn

Greek Islands

HAMBURGERS, ETC.

The Brassary
• Charlie Beinlich's
Chicago Claim
   Company
• Comeback Inn
Fritz, That's It!

The Great Gritzbe's
   Flying Food Show
• Hackney's
Hotspur's
Mel Markon's
• Melvin's

• Oak Tree
• The Other Side
• Punchinello's
R. J. Grunts

HUNGARIAN

Epicurean

INDIAN

• Bengal Lancers
Gaylord India
   Restaurant

• Taj Mahal

ITALIAN

• Armando's
• Barone's
• Cas and Lou's
• Cesar's
Club El Bianco

Del Rio
Doro's
Febo
• Gennaro's
Giannotti's

Italian Village (The
   Florentine Room)
Lawrence of Oregano
• Martini's
Trattoria Gallo

JAPANESE

Benihana of Tokyo
Dai-Ichi

Ichiban of Chicago
• Kiyo's

Ron of Japan

JEWISH

• The Bagel
• Batt's Mama Restaurant

Zweig's Restaurant and
   Delicatessen

KOREAN

- Dae Ho
- Garden of Happiness
- Sam Mee

LATE NIGHT SNACKS

Dingbat's
Four Torches
Mel Markon's

Myron and Phil's Steak
and Lobster House

- North Star Inn
The Pump Room

MANDARIN

The Abacus
Dragon Inn North

- House of Hunan
- Peking Duckling House

- Yu-Lin's Chinese
Dumpling House

MEXICAN

Cafe Azteca
- La Choza

La Margarita
Meson del Lago

Mi Casa-Su Casa
Su Casa

PANCAKES

- Walker Bros. Original
Pancake House

PERUVIAN

- El Inca

PIZZA

- Gino's East
- Giordano's

- Home Run Inn
Lou Malnati's Pizzeria

- Nancy's
Pizzeria Due

POLISH

- Warsaw Restaurant

POLYNESIAN

Kahala Terrace
Kon-Tiki Ports

Shanghai Lil's

Trader Vic's

SCANDINAVIAN

Ann Sather's

SEAFOOD

- Barney's Market Club
  Cape Cod Room
  Don's Fishmarket and
  Provision Company
- L'Epuisette
- French Port

Fulton Street Fishery
  and Market
- Half Shell
  Ireland's
  Jonathan Livingston
  Seafood

King's Wharf
Oscar's
Shrimp Walk
Slicker Sam's
Tango
The Waterfront

SERBIAN

- Miomir's Serbian Club
- Zlata's Belgrade
  Restaurant

SOUL

- Gladys' Luncheonette

Queen of the Sea

STEAK, PRIME RIB OR RIBS

Al Farber's Steak Room
- The Cart
  Eli's, The Place for
  Steak
- Embers

Gene and Georgetti's
Lawry's The Prime Rib
- Miller's Steak House
  Myron and Phil's Steak
  and Lobster House

The Prime House
That Steak Joynt
Tony's Steak House

THAI

- Bangkok House

297

DINNER PRICE RANGE INDEX

Bullets (•) indicate restaurants listed in the Short Takes section.

INEXPENSIVE—UP TO $6
PER PERSON

Ann Sather's
- The Bagel
- Bangkok House
The Brassary
Café Metropole
- Charlie Beinlich's
Chicago Claim
Company
- La Choza
- Comeback Inn
La Creperie
- Dae Ho
Dianna's Restaurant
Opaa

Gaylord India
Restaurant
- Gennaro's
- Giordano's
- Gladys' Luncheonette
Greek Islands
- Hamburger Hamlet
- Home Run Inn
Ichiban of Chicago
Lou Malnati's Pizzeria
The Magic Pan
Creperie
- Mediterranean House
- Melvin's

- Nancy's
The Nite-N-Gale
- Oak Tree
Les Oeufs
Pizzeria Due
La Poêle d'Or
- Punchinello's
Queen of the Sea
R. J. Grunts
- The Silo
- Valley Lodge
- Walker Bros. Original
Pancake House
Zweig's Restaurant and
Delicatessen

LOW-MODERATE—$6–$8.95
PER PERSON

- Barone's
- Batt's Mama Restaurant
- Bengal Lancers
Berghoff Restaurant
Beverly House
- Binyon's
- Black Forest
Brown Bear
Cafe Azteca
Cantonese Cafe
- Cas and Lou's
Casbah II
- Cesar's
Court House
Dai-Ichi
Del Rio

Dragon Inn North
E'La Cum Inn
Epicurean
Febo
- Les Fontaines Rouges
Fritz, That's It!
- Garden of Happiness
- Gino's East
The Great Gritzbe's
Flying Food Show
- Hackney's
- Half Shell
Hans' Bavarian Lodge
Homestead
Hotspur's
Ignatz and Mary's

Grove Inn
Indian Trail
Jasand's
Jonathan Livingston
Seafood
Kahala Terrace
- Kiyo's
Klas
Lawrence of Oregano
- Maison Michele
- Martini's
Mel Markon's Zanadu
- The Mezzanine
Mi Casa-Su Casa
- Middle Eastern Gardens
The Milk Pail

298

- Mushroom and Sons, Ltd.
  Oscar's
- The Other Side
- Sam Mee
- San Pedro

Shrimp Walk
Slicker Sam's
Su Casa
- Taj Mahal
- Town and Country

- Village Tavern
- Warsaw Restaurant
- Wing Yee's
- Zlata's Belgrade Restaurant

HIGH-MODERATE—$9–$12 PER PERSON

The Abacus
Al Farber's Steak Room
Allgauer's Fireside
- Armando's
- Barney's Market Club
Benihana of Tokyo
The Blackhawk
Cafe Bohemia
- Cafe La Cave
Candlelight Dinner Playhouse
Cape Cod Room
- The Cart
Chef Alberto's
Club El Bianco
Country Inn of Northbrook
- Country Squire
Dingbat's
Don's Fishmarket and Provision Company
Eli's, The Place for Steak
- El Inca
- Ember's
Eugene's
Farmer's Daughter

Four Torches
- French Port
Fu-Lama Gardens
Fulton Street Fishery and Market
- The Gallery
Gene and Georgetti's
Giannotti's
- Gordon
Grassfield's International Restaurant
- Hearthfare
- House of Hunan
- Hugo's
Ireland's
Italian Village (The Florentine Room)
- Jacques'
King's Wharf
Kon-Tiki Ports
Lawry's The Prime Rib
Lee's Canton Cafe
La Margarita
- The Mavin
Meson del Lago
- Miller's Steak House
- Miomir's Serbian Club

- Mon Petit
Myron and Phil's Steak and Lobster House
Nielsen's
- North Star Inn
- Peking Duckling House
Plentywood Farm
The Prime House
Regal Court
Ron of Japan
Sage's East
Seven Eagles
Shanghai Lil's
- Squash Blossom
Tango
That Steak Joynt
Tony's Steak House
Top of the Hilton
Trader Vic's
Trattoria Gallo
The Waterfront
- Wing Hoe
- Wrigley Building Restaurant
- Yu-Lin's Chinese Dumpling House

EXPENSIVE—OVER $12 PER PERSON

Arnie's
The Atrium
The Bakery
The Barn of Barrington
The Bird
Le Bon Vivant
- Byron

- Cafe de Paris
Camellia House and Terrace Lounge
La Cheminée
Chez Paul
The Connoisseur's Dining Room

The Consort
The Cottage
Cricket's
Doro's
- L'Epuisette
Le Festival
Fond de la Tour

DINNER PRICE RANGE INDEX